BE SCARED OF EVERYTHING

EVERYTHING

HORROR ESSAYS

PETER COUNTER

BE SCARED OF EVERYTHING

HORROR ESSAYS

PETER COUNTER

Invisible Publishing
Halifax & Prince Edward County

Library and Archives Canada Cataloguing in Publication

Title: Be scared of everything : horror essays / Peter Counter.

Names: Counter, Peter, 1987- author.

Identifiers: Canadiana (print) 20200289896 | Canadiana (ebook) 20200290088 | ISBN 9781988784564 (softcover) | ISBN 9781988784625 (HTML)

Subjects: LCSH: Counter, Peter, 1987- | LCSH: Horror in mass media. | LCSH: Horror films—History and criticism. | LCSH: Horror television programs—History and criticism. | LCSH: Horror tales—History and criticism. | LCSH: Horror. | LCGFT: Essays.

Classification: LCC P96.H65 C68 2020 | DDC 700/.4164—dc23

Edited by Andrew Faulkner
Cover and interior design by Megan Fildes | Typeset in Laurentian
With thanks to type designer Rod McDonald

Invisible Publishing is committed to protecting our natural environment. As part of our efforts, both the cover and interior of this book are printed on acid-free 100% post-consumer recycled fibres.

Printed and bound in Canada

Invisible Publishing | Halifax & Prince Edward County
www.invisiblepublishing.com

Published with the generous assistance of the Canada Council for the Arts, the Ontario Arts Council, and the Government of Canada.

  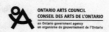 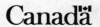

ON NOMENCLATURE

The names and identifying details of the humans mentioned in this book have been changed to protect their privacy, with the exception of public figures and consenting persons.

The names of the demons mentioned in this book have remained unchanged. Read aloud at your own risk.

For my brother Nick.
For my partner Emma.
Do what thou wilt.

CONTENT NOTES

These content notes are made available so readers can inform themselves; some readers may also consider these notes to be spoilers. This book includes references to self-harm, suicide, gun violence, and post-traumatic stress disorder (PTSD).

INTERVIEWS WITH MY FAMILY OUIJA BOARD

Jackie placed a glass of tap water on the bookshelf, put a dark stone on the ledge, and I lit incense on the table behind us. Aside from the single naked light bulb above the old coffee table, the glow of a wood stove provided most of our light. The four elements, all in their right places—water in the north, fire in the south, air in the east, and earth in the west—were supposed to protect us from what came next. Jackie joined my brother, our mother, Emma, and me, surrounding the Ouija board.

"I'm sorry," said Jackie, my brother's partner. This was her first Christmas with us in the small, lonely house on the bay. "This is serious for me."

We took turns pairing off and conducting the ritual: placing two fingers from each hand at the base of a teardrop-shaped planchette, we rotated the cursor three times and asked, "Is anybody there?"

That's how we got the first communications. Initials and ages for Jackie's dead relatives, something that called itself Frudmug, and an entity named Devur that told us about Devon who lives in Heaven and listens to you when "you syn."

When I paired with my mom after those initial summonings, kneeling next to each other, something changed. She asked the first question, usually answered with a hissing slide of the planchette to the top left corner of the board where "YES" is printed, but instead the pointer moved directly forward, encircling the game's title.

"Do you have a message for someone in this room?" asked Mom.

Yes, said the board. Then it spelled her name.

"What is your message?"

I will see you.

"Where will I see you?"

Where you wish.

"Who is this message from?" I asked.

You.

The words were agreeable. At least, that's how Mom read them. After the family seance ended, we disassembled the protective circle, and Jackie had us take a moment to offer silent gratitude for the elements. I later found Mom standing in the kitchen alone.

"It makes sense the message was so strong and clear," she said. "I think it remembered me. It used to be my board, back in the sixties."

Fifty years before the board talked to her in Jackie's circle of protection, only a half-hour drive from where our ritual took place, Mom was a preteen at the Central Wire Christmas party. Her dad, my opa, worked for Central Wire as a diamond die polisher, and every year the tradesmen and their families celebrated the holidays at Farrell Hall, a community centre that was used for mass on Sundays. When Santa arrived at the party and passed out presents to the kids, he handed little Trudy Zegger, my future mother, a Ouija board.

Unwrapping her present and lifting the lid off the box, Trudy found a grey-brown particle board with a large sticker on its front to make it look wooden. The words "YES" and "NO" were printed in the top left and right corners, next to illustrations of the sun and moon that looked down on the alphabet, which was presented in two curved rows that arch above the numbers zero through nine. The bottom of the board said "GOOD BYE," and at the very top was the name of the game—Ouija.

My family Ouija board was made in Canada, but the name and its distinct markings are trademarks of the Parker Brothers Game Company of Salem, Massachusetts. I love this detail because it creates such a wonderful contradiction: an occult object used for divination linked by intellectual property law to a place synonymous with witchcraft, and industrially manufactured en masse by a company synonymous with the brazen commercialization of the 1960s board game industry. It's not an ancient artifact, it's a toy freckled with copyright and registered trademark symbols. The planchette is made of beige plastic, with little felt pads under its feet. But that just makes it all the creepier when it works.

Trudy's initial attempts to use the board with her older sister failed to summon anything that knew how to spell. But eventually, the planchette started to answer yes or no questions.

"When I asked who it was, it spelled Rory," she told me, decades later. "After that, I often thought of Rory out there in the spirit world."

She played Ouija at pyjama parties, but as the late sixties became the mid-seventies, spiritualism gave way to plain old hanging out. Trudy loitered on Main Street, passing time in cars. She went to house parties and got really into skiing. By the time board games saw a popular resurgence in the eighties, she was in college, living on her own. Far away from the mystifying oracle stored at her parents' place, she played Pictionary instead of talking to the dead.

I found the Ouija board in my grandmother's attic a few months after she died from cancer. In life, she went by Corrie, short for Corinthia, but I knew her as Oma. Mom sat with her when she passed, in the TV room of her house deep in Ontario's Lanark Highlands, where the human population is vastly outnumbered by gasoline-green hummingbirds and moths the size of your hand. On the phone, Mom described her own mother's moment of death as a gift. A rare experience of receiving every last moment of company Oma had before suddenly being alone in a room, acutely aware of the unseen exits surrounding us. On a sweltering June afternoon, my family sorted through all the belongings that hadn't been catalogued in her will. That's what brought me into the crawl space.

A metal chain tapped against a lonely incandescent bulb dangling from the cramped room's ceiling. I leafed through stacks of old newspapers and magazines, looking for anything with historical novelty, maybe a local newspaper reporting on the Kennedy assassination, the moon landing, or the Cuban Missile Crisis. Lifting a stack of stale yellow editions of the *Perth Courier*, I uncovered the board, sitting face up in its lidless box. The room seemed to dim. I heard a buzzing in my ears. Worried it was the beginning of heatstroke, I grabbed the board and turned to leave, only to recoil from the light bulb, now covered in bloated flies, crawling over each other and falling to the wood floor with a gentle *tap-tap-tap-tap*.

I kept the board. For years, it moved with me from apartment to apartment, never leaving the blue Rubbermaid container I transported it in, until one day, when I felt fully grieved over Oma, I unpacked it and hung the beautiful game board on the wall in my apartment.

"Why are you doing this?" asked Mikaela.

"I'm not moving it," I said. "I wouldn't do that to you."

Still, the planchette slid, hissing as it finished spelling the name of her long-time crush. The line of questioning was classic Ouija. After introducing itself as Oculus, the entity offered information about who Mikaela was going to marry. I met the guy once and knew it was complicated. I'm not a monster.

"Look," I said. "The easy answer is you're moving it but you don't know it."

"It's your subconscious," said Emma, who prefers transcribing spiritual communications, since partaking in them causes her to become light-headed and nauseous.

The secular explanation to Ouija is ideomotor response. Essentially, it's a type of automatic writing powered by a feedback loop between your eyes, your subconscious mind, and the board. You ask a question with the expectation of having the answer spelled out and, as it is revealed letter by letter, your brain starts puzzle-solving and providing the subsequent characters. The effect is uncanny, and sometimes it feels like the board is reading your mind as the planchette drags your hands around the alphabet. At its best, the experience spurs self-reflection and an examination of the narratives we trace for ourselves. Self-improvement, contemplation, and contentment are the rewards of rationalist approaches to divination. Of course, many people believe it is a conduit to the afterlife—an instant messenger for spooks, spectres, and ghosts that you can buy for twenty bucks at a toy store, appropriate for ages eight and up.

Three years later, Mikaela once again asked the oracle about the person she'd marry. The entity we contacted claimed to be older than names, and said within twelve months of the current Ouija session she would meet a man named Henry in a pet store and marry him. Looking at the seance transcripts side by side, the only consistent through line is the ongoing marriage story Mikaela brings to each encounter. She asks the same questions, gets different answers, and finds a personal truth by carrying the original narrative forward. Now, free of her previous fate of a complicated marriage to a complicated crush, she's taking a second glance at every pet store she passes, hoping to meet Henry.

Regardless of your spiritual paradigm, Ouija is powerful. Playing the game can uncover forgotten truths. Some studies even show that the boards improve test scores when consulted on world geography assessments. Beseeching entities from beyond can imbue your life with meaning, change your behaviour, channel your obsession, and spur you to action. Ouija, therefore, can be dangerous.

The protective circle Jackie assembles during our winter sessions near the wood stove might seem excessive to non-spiritualists. I never took such precautions and haven't been possessed by the demon Pazuzu or victimized by a poltergeist. But that's not the kind of thing she's worried about.

"What if it pretends to be someone you know for the purposes of manipulation?" she asks.

I look to Nick. We're both thinking about the first and only time he and I queried the board together. Writing an article for a popular technology website about online Ouija boards, I had invited my brother to use the real one I found in Oma's attic as a control. The idea was to figure out how real Ouija felt. Emma was there, as always, to transcribe.

First, we conducted the seance with our eyes closed, to see if it could spell things without our help. The planchette moved on its own, sliding from letter to letter with forceful intention, but inevitably spelling out gibberish. Our second attempt, with eyes open, was more successful.

We circled the cursor three times and asked, "Is anybody there?"

Yes.

"What is your name?"

Corrie.

Before the planchette got to the *e*, tears filled my eyes. A knot in my throat stifled my follow-up question. I glanced at Nick and saw him crying too. Our oma's name, spelled out on the Ouija board from her attic. Once the shock subsided, we continued to question it, whether to prove to ourselves it was just our subconscious or to confirm her identity, I don't know.

"Are you with Opa?"

No.

"Is Opa in Heaven?"

No.

"Is Heaven real?"

Yes.

"Is Opa in Hell?"

Corrie communicated clearly and quickly, outlining a dark story of love failing to transcend life. But the cruelty of being told our grandfather was suffering put us on the defensive. We began to interrogate the entity.

"Oma, when were you born?"

1913.

"Where were you from on Earth?"

Jutland.

Those answers didn't line up. That birthdate would make her too old, and she was definitely not from Denmark, no matter how liberally you interpreted the question. We said goodbye to the thing with Oma's name and chalked up the unsettling interactions to our lingering remorse that we never really knew her as well as we should have.

Recounting the story to Jackie, the believer, gives it a new and sinister weight. What if, using the board irresponsibly, we summoned an adversary that used our narratives to warp what connection remained between us and our dead relatives, severing us from our intergenerational sense of identity? And in the end, is that demonic intervention better or worse than the alternate explanation that we tortured ourselves with guilt and regret? Within us or without us, our narrative seeped through the empty space between the characters on the Ouija board, forcing us to square with that deepest human vulnerability: questioning. Raw with renewed grief, we were ready to believe anything, so we followed the hissing plastic planchette as it reanimated our dead grandmother one letter at a time.

CELEBRATION OF LIFE

> "In the sweat of thy face thou shalt eat bread,
> till thou return to the ground; for out of it
> wast thou taken; for dust thou art, and unto
> dust thou shalt return."—Genesis 3:19

They say you don't know what you've got till it's gone, but that doesn't really apply to life as a whole. We live in the middle of a story, ignorant of our beginning and ending, bordered by the dual abysses of pre-birth and death. Life is all we have and, because we can't contrast our experience with its absence, its value is unknowable. That's what makes life a horror show.

The best horror stories don't take us into the truly unknown. Instead, they show us the limits of sensory experience, making us aware of the border between humanity and naught so we can better appreciate our toil, anguish, and frailty. Like life, horror begins with oblivion, is animated by human resistance to that terrible lifelessness, and finally urges us to accept death as inevitable.

The first act of a horror story reminds us that we can be annihilated. It presents us with ruin: an overgrown graveyard, an abandoned house, the eroded remains of a once great city, a corpse—anything that evokes futility. The titular mansion from William Hope Hodgson's *The House on the Borderland* is abandoned when two editors discover it. The narrator of H. P. Lovecraft's *At the Mountains of Madness* arrives at the headquarters of an Antarctic expedition only to find "frightfully mangled" human and canine remains, the camp's scientific implements and resources wasted on bloody human vacancy. In *Scream*, Drew Barrymore, despite her high billing and prominent position on the movie poster, is transformed from babysitter to tree ornament before the title card. In all of these cases, something had a function and then, thanks to the absence of life, it's subject to weather.

Under that shadow of human erosion in act one, every subsequent human action in a horror story becomes exultant, because nothing says "I love life" like desperately clinging to it as you hide, cry, and bleed. Horror protagonists assert authority by applying human reason and ingenuity to their dire circumstances, even when said circumstances defy any rational explanation. In *Aliens*, humanity sends the marine corps to fix an elemental problem by deploying high-tech weaponry and military tactics. In *The Ring*, tape dubbing is used to appease the vengeful spirit of a drowned girl who kills the viewers of her haunted VHS chain letter. In *End of Days*, Arnold Schwarzenegger literally tries to murder the actual devil with a grenade launcher. Countless humans self-mutilate to keep their lives in the *Saw* films, because digging out your own eye to retrieve a surgically implanted key that can remove the reverse bear trap in your mouth is apparently preferable to whatever awaits those poor souls who don't have the grit to maim themselves. Given the gruesome means by which horror protagonists are willing to suffer as they flee death, it's indisputable that they adore living.

Even boring lives are worth celebrating. In M. Night Shyamalan's *The Sixth Sense*, Bruce Willis plays the rare character who is both annihilated in act one and resists ruination in act two. Famously, after being shot to death in his own bedroom, Willis's character, Malcolm Crowe, is unable to move on. He wants to live so badly that he remains on Earth, repressing knowledge of his ghostly status. Crowe continues to work as a child psychologist, attends dinners with his wife, who he believes is having an affair, and generally endures a dull, angry life punctuated by the occasional moment of low-key creepiness.

Crowe's inability to fully pass away in *The Sixth Sense* illustrates horror's innate joie de vivre. Even a shitty, lonely life is preferable to death because at least it's known to us. Stories function through empathy, and we can't empathize with the dead. That's why, when Willis's character completes the horrific arc by accepting that he must let go of his familiar existence, he just disappears into white light. Shyamalan is confronted by the same border as Malcolm Crowe—the end of knowable human experience—and so must stop short of the unimaginable. Even our wildest inventions are confined to what our five living senses can transmit.

Acceptance of oblivion is where horror ends. It can't go further because the shape of horror is universal and analogous to life. Even if we escape Jason Voorhees, Michael Myers, or Freddy Krueger; even if we kill the aliens, murder the devil, or wash away the curse of the evil videotape; even if we cling to our crumbling grey life and keep our child psychology practice afloat, death eventually finds us.

A WORLD MADE OF TRAIN TRACKS

Have you heard the one about the waiting drifters?

Vladimir and Estragon are waiting for someone named Godot. That's the entire plot of Samuel Beckett's absurdist play *Waiting For Godot*. Godot never comes, so they continue to wait, killing time with jokes and musings and theories as to what exactly could be the holdup. That's the nature of waiting. It's passive and violent. Thinking about the future, forgetting the past. Aging in situational stasis.

Other people pass by while the men wait for Godot and the day wanes. They think maybe tomorrow their existential queue will end. But tomorrow becomes today, and it's the exact same as yesterday. The same jokes, the same musings, the same passersby. And then Vladimir snaps. How long have they been waiting? How much longer will they wait? How many times has he lived this loop of quotidian japery?

His moment of lucidity crests on a wave of guilt. "Was I sleeping while others suffered?" he asks. "Am I sleeping now?"

His awareness is intoxicating, motivating, but ultimately nothing more than another frantic type of waiting. So Vladimir rejoins Estragon in their daily pantomime, trapped in their story about nothing.

Have you heard the one about Salem, Massachusetts?

In the 1690s, the town was swept up in a mass delusion that the devil walked among its citizens, making them sign his book. Over two hundred people were accused of this divine treachery. Nineteen were sentenced to death by hanging.

Fourteen women and five men were killed this way. But one of the most famous Salem executions isn't included in those grisly statistics: the pressing of Giles Corey. Corey was brought to a field and laid down under a plank upon which stones were stacked. The monument grew higher and higher, but Corey remained silent in his crushing pain, only making a peep when asked to plead guilty to the charge of witchcraft. His accusers demanded his plea three times over two days. "More weight" was his only response.

Salem is a strange place. Halloweentown by another name, where the main street is lined with spooky souvenir shops, bookstores with witch trial transcripts displayed in the windows, and drugstores that seem to perpetually sell jack-o-lantern candies. It has the best cemeteries, the kind with slate headstones eroded by the corrosive ocean air. It has the worst tourist traps posing as museums: repurposed churches filled with clothing-store mannequins draped in approximate period garb, lit by stage lights as the tape recording of a man reciting historical bullet points plays over the PA system. Admission is twenty dollars. Photography is prohibited.

If, like my partner Emma and I, you find yourself killing time in Salem on Easter Sunday as you await the start of your 7:00 p.m. ghost walk, your best bet is to stroll the main street, looking for anything at all to make the train ride from Boston worthwhile. You will enter a store run by real Wiccans and buy a "good intention" for your witchy friend. The young man who takes your money will wish you well in the most genuine way a stranger can. Then your luck will change. All the doors that once seemed closed will open to you, and as you enter one—a Harry Potter store that sells Hogwarts robes, custom wands, and officially licensed butterbeer—the wild-looking man with glasses and long grey hair at the back will say, "Emma and Peter?"

And you'll feel like magic is real. You will feel chosen and special. *Finally*, you'll think. *I always knew my life was a ghost story*. But the man will introduce himself as Crash, tell you about the episode of *Ghost Hunters* he was on, and confirm that this is where your haunted walking tour will start in an hour and a half. Crash will recommend the Beerworks for dinner, and you'll eat a delicious meal under the green glow of a neon light shaped like the Wicked Witch of the West.

On the ghost walk, April's full pink moon will rise over a graveyard, and your tour guide, who left his family dinner to teach you about history, will take you to the memorial: a grove contained by a short stone wall. He will tell you to look down, and you will see, under your feet, words carved into the ground. The testimony of the people killed here so long ago.

You will think about the distance between you and that terrible event. The distance between you and all terrible events. You will think about innocents suffering and you will want to cry.

Have you heard the one about the Girl Guides on the tracks?

Lindsey's summer camp counsellors told her about a Girl Guide troop who'd attended the year before. On the final day, when the parents came to pick up their little cookie-selling children, three girls couldn't be found. Moms and dads looked through the cabins alongside troop leaders—in closets, under beds, behind big trees—and found nothing. They called the police, whose search led them to nearby train tracks. Blood, skin, organs, and bone fragments were spread like jam across iron rails and wooden planks. Some maniac had abducted the Girl Guides in the night, tied them up, and left them in the path of a freight train. That was the story the adults told Lindsey, so that's the story Lindsey told Emma and the other girls at her sleepover.

Emma's mom picked her up from the slumber party before bedtime, not because of Lindsey's story, but because Emma had a syndrome: she was too anxious to sleep in the presence of other children. Home in her own bed, staring at the glow-in-the-dark star stickers on her ceiling, she heard the whistle of a locomotive passing through the nearby CN Railway corridor. At that point in her life, she couldn't possibly know that the distant piping wasn't a locomotive conscripted into the murder of girls like her.

As the train continued its nocturn, Emma imagined an alternate reality. Her alternate mom arrived to pick her up from alternate Lindsey's house but couldn't find the other Emma. They looked everywhere a little girl could fit, triple-checking dangerous spaces like the clothes dryer and car trunk, but she was bound up on a set of train tracks, far from safety, shivering under the Milky Way and waiting for the deafening arrival of the train.

Emma didn't sleep that night. She thought about all the trains, all over the world, and how helpless they were to stop themselves from mutilating innocent people trapped in their way.

Sometimes the world feels made of train tracks, a planet-sized rubber-band ball of iron, spikes, and wood, devilish engines, chugga-chugga-chugging along. Each of us anticipating the moment that distant whistle becomes a rumble, becomes obliterating locomotion, becomes our untimely end. There is no escape from suffering, even behind closed eyes. There is only the wait.

PLEASE ADD ME TO YOUR
ZOMBIE SURVIVAL NETWORK

Gwen asked if I'd kill her. I had to think about it. The two of us sat in a theatre in downtown Toronto, paper programs in our laps. Black walls, black curtains, black metal legs supporting grey plastic chairs, all lit by the white glow of the house lights. The kind that bring out the red in your cheeks. Blood vision.

"I could do it," I said. "Emotionally, I think I could."

I took silent inventory. With me, I had a messenger bag containing a notebook and a bottle of red wine. The pockets of my jeans were empty, save for my old leather wallet. My keys, a ticket stub, a small black cellphone, and a handful of unused tissues cluttered the various compartments of my theatre-school-grade corduroy blazer. I was unarmed. "But I don't think I have anything that would really help me with the dirty work."

"You can kill a zombie with your hands," she said. "You do karate."

I pictured the hypothetical scenario. A raspy moan, Gwen's eyes covered in the instant cataracts of undeath, mouth gaping with angry eyebrows. She'd go for my exposed flesh first, probably—my face and neck. I'd guard myself, either through the automatic reflex of a karate high block or by cartoonishly palming her head to keep her at bay, the Bugs Bunny to her flesh-eating chicken hawk. Honestly considering my abilities and the implements at hand, I couldn't imagine any way to remove Gwen's head or destroy her brain.

"I don't know. Is karate even enough?" I said. "I'd have to run."

Gwen raised an eyebrow. People crowded near the edge of the stage, looking up at the risers, squinting and doing basic math, trying to find a place to squeeze their party in with the rest of us spectators.

"Let's say you had something," she said. "Let's say you had a bat or a shovel. Let's say you could definitely do it."

I asked where she was headed with this. Judging by the densely packed seating, we didn't have a ton of time for zombie talk before the curtain's rising.

"Okay," she said. "If I attack you first, having not bitten anyone to spread the zombie virus, and you karate me back to death right here, will anyone believe you did it to save the world? Or will they all think you're a murderer?"

Everyone in the theatre sat, shifting, murmuring, and turning off their phones. The collective noun is audience, crowd. But I was thinking about hordes.

"I'm just saying, the smart thing to do is let the situation get a little out of hand," said Gwen. "Not too out of hand. Not *28 Days Later* out of hand. Just enough that tomorrow's headlines contain the word 'infected' instead of 'murder.'"

The lights began to dim. For a moment, a couple hundred bodies sat in utter darkness.

"This is probably a good time to tell you I'm coming down with a fever," Gwen whispered. "Remember, let it get a little out of hand."

"What if you bite me?"

"I don't care, I'm already dead."

We talk about zombies to talk about each other. In pubs, at parties, in theatre audiences waiting for plays to start, we imagine the undead uprising in present tense. In a hypothetical survival scenario, your interests, obsessions, and special skills take on heavy significance. The summer job you had landscaping could make you the chainsaw-wielding splatterpunk who saves her friends in a cloud of gas fumes and blood. Time served on your high school baseball team might elevate you to the José Bautista of blunt-force head removal. Practical firearms experience accrued on a hunting trip with your uncle can cast you as Annie Oakley in St. John's Revelation.

As an old millennial, of the cohort who started surfing the web around age nine, I learned to write personality profiles for my digital self before learning the cardinal directions in school. Chat rooms, pop culture forums, and instant messenger programs like ICQ required me to socialize without a body. Like other people my age, I built digital avatars out of song lyrics and self-portraits. Screen name, age, country, favourite movie, favourite song, inspirational quote, uploaded image—disclosure of this data is an essential first step in communication for people who came of age during the rise of Internet society, who spend most of our social lives in collectively imagined non-corporeal spaces. That's why zombies are such an appealing conversation topic. A zombie apocalypse discussion is profile building for the meatspace. Agreeing to a set scenario with high stakes and an internal logic established by film, TV, video games, and past conversations, we define ourselves in opposition to the undead. We laugh, we drink, and together we agree that in a world consumed by viral walking death, the people we know and love will survive by virtue of our describable utility.

Because zombies are non-human, non-living, and unable to list their hobbies in order of practicality, the shambling corpses are barely part of the conversations they inspire. Generally, actual zombie talk begins and ends with taxonomy. If we're really going to discuss a survival plan, we need to know what kind of monsters we're running from. Are we dealing with classic slow zombies or a newfangled strain of rage zombies that can run? Do their bites quickly transform living victims into card-carrying members of Club Zed or are we imagining a situation in which infection only means resurrection after a less supernatural death? These questions, along with the origin of the zombification vector— biomedical research gone wrong, trendy anti-aging cream applied too liberally, a novel coronavirus—help define the survival logic of the discussion. Everything else is about being alive together and staying that way.

Your zombie apocalypse profile is constantly changing with your interests, attitudes, and values. Physically active hobbies usually take up the first bits of conversation. The knee-jerk reaction is that a zombie apocalypse privileges those who can pulverize a skull. But close-contact melee with zombies is a losing battle. It's like beating back the rising tide with a crowbar.

It only takes a few minutes to realize that survival is about creatively co-operating to make the best of the worst possible situation. Identifying friends and acquaintances with first-aid training leads to recollected adventures in babysitting. Finding shelter and foraging for food evoke shared memories of hiking, camping, and hunting. At one point, someone inevitably suggests commandeering a boat and waiting out the apocalypse on the water. This person will share stories of sailing, powerboating, or working at a marina over teenage summers. The conversation will progress, trust will emerge, and those of us with chronic medical conditions will ask if the survival party minds stopping at a pharmacy to loot EpiPens, inhalers, or insulin.

I am a lifelong martial artist, which usually puts me on guard duty. I graduated university with a performance-heavy theatre degree, which is generally thought to be use-less unless you count the fact that it's probably the reason we're talking about zombies in the first place. I have asthma and a chronic back injury. My favourite band is the White Stripes. My favourite film is *The Blair Witch Project*. My inspirational quote is a haiku by Kobayashi Issa: "O snail / Climb Mount Fuji, / But slowly, slowly!" Please add me to your zombie survival network.

Zombies are the monster we talk about because the stories that focus on them use the language of breaking news and scientific discovery in a bid for verisimilitude. Mysticism, meet biohazard, meet broken quarantine, meet twenty-four-hour news coverage and presidential addresses and riots. Exorcists, meet researchers. Demons, meet germs.

I was in Grade 9 math class on September 11, 2001. My teacher, Mr. Leonard, didn't tell my class why school was suddenly cancelled, so it was only after being ferried home on a school bus, turning on the TV, and flipping to the all-news channel that I became aware of the mayhem. Sitting alone on the dusty grey couch in our sunlit family room, still wearing my school uniform, I saw the images we've all watched on repeat. Planes flying into skyscrapers. People jumping from windows. Buildings I'd only ever seen depicted in fiction collapsing. After the initial impacts, in that uneasy time when any horrible thing seemed possible, almost every channel replayed the foot-age for viewers just tuning in.

Something important and world-changing is happening, I thought, and it made me sick with guilt. Watching the news that day was the first time I understood the World Trade Center buildings as real, and as I saw them tumble over and over, I felt a mortifying, horrendous thrill. *This could be the end*. I felt flattered to be alive, witnessing violent history. The newscasts flashing on my family's tube television taught me the vernacular of a world falling apart.

The zombie films of the early 2000s adopted the visual language of terrorist attack coverage as a shorthand to illustrate how the real undead threat ought to feel. Danny Boyle's seminal *28 Days Later*, released only thirteen months after the Twin Tower catastrophe, begins with the images of violent news footage prior to the film's inciting outbreak. Its second sequence, which takes place after the evacuation of Great Britain, features actor Cillian Murphy silently walking through a decimated London, juxtaposing recognizable landmarks like Big Ben with the post-9/11 iconography of a wounded metropolis, most notably a makeshift memorial wall covered in drawings, letters, and photos of victims. The 2004 remake of *Dawn of the Dead*, written and directed by superhero filmmakers James Gunn and Zack Snyder, respectively, goes all the way with its allegory, using staged news footage of military deployments firing automatic weapons into swarms of bodies, and White House press briefings in which politicians are unable to confirm whether the victims of a spreading pathogen are in fact living or dead.

I'm not saying 9/11 invented the zombie apocalypse. That's reductive. But it did familiarize the media language of mass mayhem that's used to make zombie outbreaks seem more realistic in entertainment. Boyle and Snyder showed me what the news coverage would look like if monsters attacked instead of Al Qaeda. Their ability to self-justify their horror brought it closer to the border of potential reality.

Two years after Snyder's *Dawn of the Dead* remake made malls the place to be for the apocalypse, zombie self-justification was bolstered even further by non-fiction. The eighth episode of the BBC documentary series *Planet Earth*, titled "Jungles," captured a real-life, albeit diminutive, zombie apocalypse in high-definition film.

"These bullet ants are showing some worrying symptoms," narrates David Attenborough over close-up shots of an insect in distress. "Spores from a parasitic fungus called Cordyceps have infiltrated their bodies and their minds." The camera follows the fate of one ant, which, compelled to climb upward by the fungal filaments nesting in its body, clamps its mandibles into the stem of a plant before its head erupts, producing a white tendril that rains spore particles on the colony below. Bullet ants caught under the falling dust are doomed to the same fate, playing host to zombie mushrooms as mycelia manipulate their nervous systems. "The fungus is so virulent," says Attenborough, "it can wipe out whole colonies of ants."

As you'd expect, Cordyceps supercharged the zombie conversations of the *Planet Earth* era. The realistic images of disaster news coverage showed us what a zombie apocalypse looked like after that first fateful bite, but until *Planet Earth*, the origin had to be speculative, some sort of fantasy virus. Cordyceps gave us a clear beginning, a real zombifying infectant only one cross-kingdom jump away from fulfilling the prophecy of our catastrophic fantasies. "Have you seen *Planet Earth*?" someone would say after the clink of pint glasses. "How about those zombie ants?" Ten minutes later, the table is three weeks into a sustainable post-apocalyptic survival plan and more intimately connected than most first cousins. In the zombie apocalypse, you build a new family.

With the missing piece of a realistic vector in place, zombie fiction finally possessed all the tools for a fully plausible secular apocalypse, leaning closer to speculation than fantasy. In 2013, video game developer Naughty Dog released *The Last of Us*, a narrative-driven experience that takes players from the eve of a human Cordyceps outbreak and the cold military response straight through to the bleak conclusion that humanity might not be worth saving. Featuring real motion-capture acting, touching voice performances, and easily the best script written for a major studio-developed video game, *The Last of Us* is overgrown with verisimilitude, achieving the exit velocity required to escape the gravity of horror genre and video game stigma.

The Last of Us, many critics argued, was not a game. One didn't so much play *The Last of Us* as they endured it. The violence was too realistic, requiring the player to murder human beings with bricks or improvised petrol bombs, for no reward other than safety; no points, just survival. *The Last of Us* aspires to realism first, horror second, and in doing so reveals how meaningless those distinctions actually are. It's the only zombie story that can make me cry in its final moments. It's about the horrible things we do for family. People we don't know might as well be bad weather. They might as well be zombies.

"I want you to cut it off," said Bruce. "Dave can use the fire axe. But I'm probably going to pass out. I think if we make a tourniquet first, that might help. But we have to cut off my arm." He looked at me from across a table covered in paper, wooden game pieces, and a map of the Royal Ontario Museum. "I show them my arm."

"Bruce shows you his arm," I confirm. "The bloody teeth marks are surrounded by dark bruising. Deep blue and black veins stretch out from the wound, almost reaching his shoulder."

As the game master of the tabletop role-playing game session, I maintained distance. The umpire and living statistical engine of the imaginary zombie apocalypse, I brought my best friends—Katie and her fiancé Dave, Emma and her pre-med student cello teacher, the soon-to-be-armless Bruce—on this field trip of nightmares. I couldn't participate in the decision. I was there to watch and roll dice—and confirm or deny potential actions while the closest thing to a doctor at our table argued for an unanesthetized amputation.

"Can't we do anything to numb the pain?" asked Katie.

"You can knock me out. Then I won't flinch."

"None of us know how to knock you out," said Emma. "This isn't TV. If we hit you in the head, you might die."

"Hold on. Hold on," said Dave, hands out over the table as if physically pushing the rising emotions down onto the game pieces. "Can I just pause for a second? Peter, we don't know enough to call these zombies. Right?"

I had to think about it. I consulted my notes. "There are similarities. Obviously."

"This is a bad idea," said Emma, sitting farther away from the table.

"Yeah, I don't want to do this," said Katie.

"It's my arm," said Bruce.

And it went on like this.

Outbreak: Undead bills itself as a zombie survival simulator. Available to order as a couple of hardcover books from one of the nerdier corners of the Internet, it's a comprehensive set of probability charts, lists, timetables, and tips on how to facilitate a fun and collaborative time imagining the end of the world. Devised by *King of the Nerds* contestant and dragon-enthusiast Ivan Van Norman, *Outbreak: Undead* is appealing because it helps apply rules to zombie apocalypse conversations. Personal profile building meets the aspirational realism of the zombie genre itself. A personality quiz translates every participant's fitness ability, emotional capacity, and mental aptitude into statistical character sheets, and the game master handles the larger narration while dice take on the role of luck.

Emma, Katie, and Dave convinced Bruce to keep his arm. Even if they conceded that they were facing off against real-deal zombies, they couldn't possibly know the underlying logic of whatever was causing Torontonians to hunger for the flesh of the living. Recognizing the zombie apocalypse is not understanding the zombie apocalypse. The mental gymnastics required to come to this conclusion still impress me—playing a game designed to simulate a zombie apocalypse, they pretended they didn't know it was the zombie apocalypse until they'd accrued enough empirical evidence to make the comparison, only to deduce that whatever they were experiencing might not be the zombie apocalypse after all. It was Olympic-level suspension of disbelief.

I designed this armageddon, so I knew that eventually the black veins would stretch all the way to Bruce's heart, killing him. And if his friends didn't destroy his brain, or remove his head, or dissolve him in acid, or do something equally obliterating, he would return, no longer Bruce but a monster with his face.

Before any of that could happen, their party was ambushed. As they attempted to escape onto Bloor Street through the broken glass of the museum entrance, three shambling ex-urbanites descended on Dave. He swung his axe; I rolled the dice. Two attackers stumbled back, but the third sunk its teeth into Dave's neck. Katie and Emma blinked back tears and Bruce's face sunk. Dave let out a deep breath. These four people had talked so many times about the undead end of the world as a hypothetical, but now words meant action, and action always means consequence. The fantasy fell apart. We only played *Outbreak:*

Undead once more after that. Then we stopped talking about zombies altogether.

Zombie talk is a way of painting our modern fears of annihilation with a bloodless coat of grey. Self-justification animates those fears, makes them shuffle, and moan, and bite. By treating the zombie apocalypse as real in our conversations, we tacitly give ourselves permission to associate real disasters like bombings, and climate change, and economic collapse with fiction. All of those real destroyers of life are, after all, what the walking dead represent. They are the things that happen to everyone else by virtue of being on the wrong side of the camera. By talking about zombies, we drag them into our world, diminishing the border between fantastical death and the chaos that could end everything right now.

As I type these words, in the spring of 2018, an Ebola outbreak is killing people in the Democratic Republic of Congo. The last time the deadly microbe claimed human lives, killing 11,359 people between 2013 and 2016, the international epidemic was reported through the comparative lens of AMC's horror serial *The Walking Dead* and resulted in viral zombie hoaxes on the Internet. My Twitter feed is filled with the images of the Congo quarantine, interspersed with news of the latest US school shooting—the third this year, which resulted in the deaths of children. Unimaginable suffering populates my computer monitor, and while it's sickening and terrifying, it only feels half real. I have a mental block filtering the news through the genre tropes of horror films that rely on the same imagery of blood, tears, and biohazard warning symbols. Real danger is tempered by fantastical excitement, and what I'm left with is a sensation of unearned safety.

I have my browser open to YouTube, playing a video of Ronald Poppo, recorded a year after he had the flesh chewed from his skull. Poppo is famous for being the homeless survivor of the Miami cannibal attack in 2012. One year before the release of *The Last of Us*, a naked Floridian by the name of Rudy Eugene accused Poppo of stealing his Bible. Eugene then beat Poppo senseless, removed his pants, and ate the unconscious man's face. A police officer shot Eugene dead, saving Poppo, but not before the cannibal consumed the poor man's eye, along with almost all the skin between his mouth and the crown of his skull.

In the video I'm watching, Ronald Poppo is playing guitar, having received medical treatment and various therapies. He has no eyes, and the smooth skin above his mouth does little to hide his bone structure. He is half skeleton, transformed by a bite. It's easier to imagine Poppo as a living reminder of a near-apocalyptic outbreak, to imagine that the police officer who shot Rudy Eugene saved the world. But as Poppo puts down his guitar and extols the virtues of the social programs that literally saved his life, he doesn't use the zed word. He is not the lone survivor of a one-man undead apocalypse. He's just a survivor. To liken his trauma to the plot of a horror film feels exploitative. It feels disrespectful. But it also feels comfortable, much more so than admitting that what he experienced was simply the chaos that permeates human existence. That at any moment, the cameras could turn to me as a naked stranger dives teeth-first into my face, or as I join the panicking masses in the aftermath of a terrorist attack perpetrated by an angry white gun owner, or as I get sick from an ancient microbe and bleed to death from the eyes, nose, and anus.

Even as I write down those potential realities, trying to imagine each one in terrible detail, they remain as hypothetical as a zombie outbreak. Technically, I am more likely to be consumed by the terrors of human conflict, with its tanks, and its bombs, and its guns. But in my head, it's all just as real as getting bitten, killed, and resurrected by my friend Gwen as we settle in to watch a play in a crowd of strangers.

THE FBI'S BASEMENT OFFICE

"I just saw a UFO," he said.

When my brother phoned at eleven in the evening, I panicked. Nick usually gives me a courtesy text before calling, so my mind went into crisis mode as I picked up the phone. I thought of potential family deaths or the kind of trauma he might come to me about first. Visions of the night he walked away from a car crash, the only one of his group of four friends still conscious, our mom's purple Acura a pile of twisted metal. I answered, bracing for the worst. But this felt like a prank. UFOs were the stuff of fantasy.

"Are you on anything?" I asked.

"I'm sober."

Even as he meticulously explained the encounter, I couldn't bring myself to accept his testimony. House-sitting for our parents, Nick had been looking out on the backyard under a deep, dark April night sky when three bright lights moving at a steady high speed converged above the in-ground pool. They stopped, according to him, snapping into place, hovering in a triangle formation before beginning to rotate. The triangle's spinning accelerated, it got smaller, and vanished.

"I got a video of it," he said, as if my disbelief radiated over the line. "Near the end. I didn't record it all since I dropped my phone."

He hung up and sent me a video over email. Sure enough, two static lights in the sky above our parents' pool were joined by a third, moving in a direct line at a speed that reminded me of a marble rolling down a slightly uneven table and stopping on a divot. They revolved on an invisible axis, just like Nick said, and disappeared.

I played it over and over, a cold dread crawling up my spine, muscles tensed ever so slightly in apprehension. My brain started doing gymnastics, trying to fit the image into a rational narrative. Consumer-grade drone technology wouldn't be available for years, so my knee-jerk reaction was to believe it was a military aircraft. Already, I was in dangerous territory, the stuff of conspiracy theory, but any alternative explanations that came to mind were even more cliché, if not any less likely to be true. Aliens. Robots. Atlanteans. I had to admit I didn't actually know enough about statistics to confidently say a secret government aircraft was any less probable than extraterrestrial visitation or the existence of a technologically sophisticated submarine species who live in a sunken city that somehow evades human detection. If this was real, whatever "real" meant in that moment, then it would change everything. After all, the existence of UFOs should unite feuding nations in shared curiosity and fear, like the ending of Alan Moore's *Watchmen*, in which a staged alien attack defuses Cold War tensions. Intelligent engineering of unknown origin is up there with climate change and pandemics on the list of big deals for the human race.

The next morning at my customer service call centre job, I read the news in between answering phones. Apparently there had been multiple UFO sightings the night before, all over Southern Ontario. But reading about the encounters in print made the proposal of flying saucers difficult to square with my fluorescent, nine-to-five present, working for an hourly wage in business-casual dress, selling tickets to the symphony. When I talked about Nick's video with my co-workers at the coffee machine, needing to share my personal connection to the news du jour, I steeped my story in a heavy broth of cynical disbelief. Only crazy people believe in UFOs, even when there's video evidence. *Especially* when there are videos. The incident felt notable and dramatic, but I wasn't ready, emotionally, to accept *The X-Files* as non-fiction.

Aired from 1993 through 2002, *The X-Files* was among the most popular American television dramas of its decade. Following the investigations of Fox Mulder and Dana Scully, two outcast FBI agents working out of the Bureau's basement office, the show was a paranormal procedural that borrowed heavily from real supernatural lore to bring a sense of uncanny verisimilitude to its episodic format. Encountering vampires, haunted dolls, the Jersey Devil, and a time warp in the Bermuda Triangle, Mulder and Scully peppered their mystery-solving banter with spooky factoids and trivia, along with a helping of fringe science that made even their goofier adventures seem just a little bit plausible. While the agents investigated every possible horror trope, sometimes twice (Scully fought off multiple Mulder doppelgängers in the nineties), they are best known as heroes tangled in an ongoing government conspiracy to prepare the Earth for colonization by alien visitors. Roughly six to eight hours of every twenty-some-thing-episode season were dedicated to a semi-serialized plot drawing from real military history and actual abduction accounts. These episodes built the popular mythology of UFOs, aliens, and evil men who smoke cigarettes in gloomy Pentagon offices while watching presidents die. The mythology is so dense, so popular, and so blended with reality that it became the main cultural touch point for UFO phenomena. Fiction co-opted the less verifiable eyewitness parts of reality to build a realistic mythos, which became the foundation for how we understand unidentified flying objects: as fantasy rather than an area of inquiry worth investigating. Mulder and Scully were science-fiction all-stars worth emulating only in allegory.

In a May 2000 *LA Times* cover story titled "Hangin' Out with Rock's Rude Boys," staff writer Geoff Boucher chronicles a day spent with Blink-182 when the band is scheduled to appear on *The Tonight Show with Jay Leno*. A case of laryngitis contracted by the band's co-frontman and bassist, Mark Hoppus, meant a last-minute set change that replaced the band's ultra-popular suicide ballad "Adam's Song" with "Aliens Exist," a Tom DeLonge-sung tune. "It's about aliens that come down to Earth and fly up your butt," DeLonge told the *LA Times*. "And it's true."

Despite DeLonge's in-your-face allegation of extraterrestrial probing, "Aliens Exist" is played deadpan on Blink-182's 1999 pop-punk landmark *Enema of the State*. The guitarist recites, "We all know conspiracies are dumb," but that doesn't stop him from abandoning the tongue-in-cheek, running-naked-through-the-street aesthetic that made his band famous. The song sounds like the frustrated confession of an obsessed young man, with nary a Uranus joke.

Fifteen years after the Jay Leno set, DeLonge's earnestness on the topic became clear when he quit the band and began pursuing ufology, writing books about alien technology and exchanging emails with US government officials like John Podesta on topics such as Area 51 and the infamous Roswell Incident. DeLonge even launched a company called To the Stars Academy of Arts & Science, a start-up dedicated to harvesting and learning from UFO technology with the aim of sparking revolutions in science, engineering, entertainment, and consciousness (while no mention of ESP research remains on the To the Stars web-site as of this writing, a 2017 preliminary offering circular archived with the US Securities and Exchange Commission references the company's research into telepathy).

DeLonge came across as ridiculous because he was acting like a character from *The X-Files*. He might as well have joined the Church of Scientology, come out as a flat-earther, or asserted that he could speak with animals like Doctor Dolittle. Of all the things a person could possibly dedicate their life to, UFO research is among the most lethal to one's public image.

But DeLonge and other ufologists and abductees should have been exonerated on December 16, 2017, when the cover story of the *New York Times* Sunday edition exposed a clandestine Department of Defense program dedicated to the study of unidentified flying objects. The Advanced Aerospace Threat Identification Program (AATIP) was started in 2007 by Democratic senator Harry Reid. Fuelled by $22 million of untraceable funding, the initiative investi-gated strange aerial phenomena that demonstrated motion capabilities far beyond the limits of human engineering and interfered with military weapons systems. Luis Elizondo, who ran the program from the Pentagon, characterized the objects as threats to national security that warranted seri-ous research and analysis.

Despite documented video evidence of silvery shapes in the sky moving at impossible speeds and pivoting with grace, military personnel rarely reported close encounters for fear of ridicule. Such stigma seems to be the root cause of the program's 2012 decommissioning. According to the *New York Times'* sources, DoD officials still independently investigate UFO reports, but they do so without depart-mental financial support. Frustrated with the continued secrecy, the defunding, and the overall lack of seriousness afforded a topic he still sees as high priority, Elizondo resigned from his government position to enter the private sector. He and two other former Pentagon officials now seek the truth alongside DeLonge at To the Stars Academy, corroborating the paranoid punk rocker's radical and fantastical worldview.

UFOs are real in the most cliché sense, which makes them nearly impossible to believe in if you didn't already entertain their existence before 2017. In borrowing from the highly stigmatized UFO sighting subculture, *The X-Files* made us associate legitimate unknown phenomena with a very good but also extremely silly television drama. Now that AATIP has been dragged into the light of day, the UFO episodes of Mulder and Scully's adventures almost play like historical fiction rather than sci-fi. Almost. Because the U in UFO is a scary U. The unidentified. The unknown. The unclassifiable.

By the end of its initial nine-season run, *The X-Files* provided answers to all of its alien mysteries. In real life, Elizondo and DeLonge don't have those answers. No one does. The narrative is unfinished, and it will remain that way if we can't accept that the pariahs weren't lying when they told us about the shining lights in the sky.

It's ironic that *The X-Files*' accuracy makes it so difficult to believe the assertions of UFO spotters. Not only did the show endeavour to portray abductees and witnesses in a sympathetic light—often to tear-jerking effect, as in the case of the recurring character Max Fenig, who endures a lifetime of torture made all the worse by society's unwillingness to accept his story—but in the show's finest hour, Season 3's "Jose Chung's 'From Outer Space,'" Mulder shares a powerful monologue about the influence of popular culture on highly stigmatized communities. Urging author Jose Chung to abandon the writing of a non-fiction book about the alleged abduction of two teenagers by a lava monster named Lord Kinbote, who hails from the inner space of the Earth's core, Mulder says:

> "You perform a disservice to a field of inquiry that has always struggled for respectability. You're a gifted writer, but no amount of talent could describe the events that occurred in any realistic vein because they deal with alternative realities that we have yet to comprehend, and when presented in the wrong way, in the wrong context, the incidents and the people involved in them can appear foolish, if not downright psychotic."

In the world of the show, Mulder is the voice of compassion. But to a viewer, every episode of *The X-Files* functions like Chung's book. Even when it's serious, the show is still fantasy—created, presented, and consumed in a reality that largely dismisses the non-religious paranormal. *The X-Files* uses its UFO mythos to teach us about faith, skepticism, human connection, and trust. But its most practical lesson, that we should take UFO sightings seriously, falls victim to our deeply ingrained reading habits regarding genre fiction. We dismiss it as an entertaining vehicle for a deeper meaning. Sci-fi isn't supposed to be literal.

Even writing this, I feel torn between what I know from the news and my expectations of reality. I've seen video evidence of a UFO. I've read the *New York Times* exposé and subsequent reports. On their own, they should provide me with enough of an informed vantage point to accept our new strange skies. But for some reason, I can't fully accept this as one of Mulder's "alternative realities." The truth is out there, and I'm filled with a DeLongean frustration that society is more concerned with the explainable Earthbound threats facing the Pentagon and the increasingly rigid lines of partisan human-on-human conflict. We should be trying to figure out this UFO thing. We should be dedicating all of our time to searching for answers to skyborne unknowns. We should unite as a species out of shared curiosity and possibly (if Elizondo is right about them being a threat) self-preservation. I should quit my job and join To the Stars—but I can't bring myself to put my money where my mouth is. Fifty-one percent of my mind thinks buying stock in DeLonge's firm would be a very funny joke, but ultimately not worth the $350 minimum price tag, despite the US military's continual validation of Tom's views. Cynicism informed by pop culture always conquers fear. My paradigm is jammed by *The X-Files*. I want to believe but can't.

TOO-LOO

Ktulu. It was a hiccup in my teenage brain. I first encountered the word among the list of track titles while reading the liner notes to the Metallica CD spinning in my stereo, sitting next to my guitar amplifier in my parents' basement. What did it mean? The song "The Call of Ktulu" started with delicate D-minor arpeggiating, quickly turned sinister, and built into a sonic dark advent—but no lyrics materialized to enlighten me. Eight minutes and fifty-three wordless seconds of ascending, guitar-driven rock culminated in an apocalyptic breakdown, only to return to the same mysterious riff from its beginning.

How do you even pronounce it? I thought. *K'tuoluo? Katuloo? Or maybe the K is silent. Tulu.* The song left me without a clue.

I told everyone the name of my favourite song was "'Call of Too-Loo' by Metallica."

"Let's start with Thoo-luh," said David, a fantasy-obsessed master of jazz performance who played axe in a Christian metal band named God's Eye View. David taught me guitar on Tuesdays after school. Sitting on a stool in his basement apartment's teaching studio, under monolithic black plastic CD towers and guitars hung on the wall like crucifixes, he opened the Metallica songbook I'd received for Christmas. Eyes wild with enthusiasm, he smiled through his brown beard. "Do you know about Lovecraft?"

Lovecraft, David said, created a pantheon of alien monsters that humans saw as evil gods, and chief among them was the subject of Metallica's song. "They spell it wrong for some reason," he said. "I'm pretty sure it's pronounced with a *th* sound at the beginning."

I learned to play the song, but the pronunciation eluded me. So when I performed the tune at a recital David arranged at a Baptist church on the edge of town, right after a highly abridged piano rendition of Beethoven's Fifth Symphony by a kid half my age, I announced my act the way David taught me, with an interdental fricative. Years later, I was living in Toronto, no longer taking guitar lessons, and the Internet had evolved enough to help me find the correct spelling via a Wikipedia entry on Metallica. "Cthulhu." Not exactly the solution to my pronunciation problem.

I turned to literature. Grabbing one of the myriad Lovecraft anthologies from my local bookstore, I devoured the fiction during a grey Toronto winter, in cafés, university common areas, and under lamplight before bed. The word "Cthulhu" was speckled throughout the prose, alongside the names of other strange gods that seemed easier to pronounce. Nyarlathotep. Azathoth. Yog-Sothoth. A completist by nature, I read the collection front to back. When I finally reached "The Call of Cthulhu," the story I expected to at least contain some kind of pronunciation key or phonetic representation of the word, I realized my years of searching were futile.

Reading Lovecraft's story, I learned the name's origin. "Cthulhu" is heard in the nightmares of sensitive artists who herald the coming of the great old one, who lies eternal, dreaming in the sunken city of R'lyeh. The name is a "chaotic sensation" that "only fancy could transmute into sound," a string of syllables the human apparatus is unable to replicate, spoken by a "voice that is not a voice." Transcribed from a memory into an imperfect phonetic representation, the word "Cthulhu" is an estimation of an unspeakable reality the artists are compelled to depict through language and craft. And they don't stop with the name: they paint the god's image, they sculpt his form—a bloated dragon with the head of a many-tentacled cephalopod. Is it such a stretch that Metallica might also attempt to communicate the unspeakable through a lyricless guitar anthem, doomed as the band may be to fail by virtue of human limitation, composing "The Call of Ktulu" to offer a glimpse of their apocalyptic vision? Unknowable.

CORPORATE PERSONHOOD

"Ripley, she doesn't have bad dreams because she's just a piece of plastic."
—Newt, *Aliens* (1986)

Violence came first. It must have, even if I can't remember it. The kind of mindless cruelty that emerges from natural systems of procreation and evolution—like how some wasps lay eggs inside paralyzed rodents so their larvae can eat their way out in a grotesque birthday celebration. Actually, come to think of it, that's almost exactly what's going on, with an extraterrestrial spin. My chest is an incubator for a xenomorph, the monster from the *Alien* film franchise.

I know how this works. At first, I'll seem fine, but then the nausea will hit. I'll heave, I'll hemorrhage, until a chitinous, snakelike creature explodes from my sternum in a shower of blood and bone fragments, hungry and squealing for release. My fate is inescapable, and I know it, so I start to come to terms with death before this scene plays out. When the hungry fledgling burrows out of my torso, my surrogate offspring will mature quickly, growing into a phallus-headed black monstrosity resembling a puma crossed with a scorpion.

There's nothing I can do now. No one ever survives the chest-burster scene. In my final moments of meta-awareness that I'm succumbing to a movie plot device, I curse the shadowy multinational conglomerate whose obsession with weaponizing xenomorphs put monsters in contact with humans in the first place.

Damn you, Weyland-Yutani, I think.
Then I wake up and scream.

The monsters in my dreams don't belong to me. They are the intellectual property of large media corporations. As a child, I had nightmares of Vigo the Carpathian, the evil fiend from *Ghostbusters 2*. I dreamed his face started pressing through the wall next to my bed, which flexed like it was made of fabric instead of drywall with dinosaurs painted on it. As a teenager, my sleep was haunted by Michael Myers, the masked murderer from the *Halloween* films. Myers chased me through the streets of Clinton, Ontario, where my granddad lived. He inevitably caught up and stabbed me to death at the base of the giant radar dish downtown. Once, I dreamed that Crash Bandicoot, the mascot for Sony PlayStation, eviscerated me with two giant razor blades in a dusty attic with a skylight and creaky wooden floorboards.

My chest-burster *Alien* dream is more common than those. I've had it my entire life, waking year after year, covered in panic-induced sweat, and jetting to the bathroom to chug cold water to try and drown the dreadful pressure in my esophagus. For the first thirty years, my slumbery scares were the property of 20th Century Fox. In 2019, Disney acquired Fox's entertainment division, effectively staking a claim on my decades of restless sleep and phantom nausea. Next time I wake from an *Alien* dream, I'll have a new company to blame: the one with the iconic mouse ears, the mother of xenomorphs, the proverbial alien queen and her puss-filled egg sac of nightmares.

Corporations are persons, according to law. They have legal rights and are treated in a similar manner to individuals when it comes to ownership of intellectual property.

Corporations have their own pronouns, referred to always as "it" in press releases. The CEO and chairpeople may speak on its behalf, but the corporation is an individual entity, not a collective.

We use anatomical language to describe corporate persons. They have branches and arms with heads and back ends. Disney and other large corporations are like colossal, invisible plant-animal hybrids, cultivating symbiotic relationships with us humans. As it grows, Disney generates new appendages, subsuming more humans into the memetic superstructure. It merges with other corporations, expanding dramatically, hoarding precious assets while shedding staff and other dead weight along the way. Merchandise is sold, language is hijacked by jargon, ideas born in human brains proliferate and are absorbed. That's how the Disney-monster came to own *Star Wars*, Marvel, and *Alien*.

In our current era, the comedies, tragedies, and hero journeys central to human self-reflection are modernized and distributed through conglomerates. Corporate persons hijacked the means through which we process hope, joy, grief, and catharsis. That's why we worship corporate-owned images: because they are the icons we use to contextualize our lives. We create fan art and adopt proprietary characters into our own personal narratives, foregoing the creation of something new and unowned in favour of iterating the property of a non-living entity, occupying our brains with Luke Skywalker, the Avengers, and Elsa from *Frozen*. Once upon a time, these creative assets were as transitory as the corporate worker. Prior to corporate personhood, an artist's work was subject to public-domain laws, meaning that after a certain period of time, the work belonged to the people who dreamed about it. But corporations are immortal and can eternally lobby for the renewal of copyright. I'll die before Disney relinquishes ownership of the baby alien continually killing me in my dreams.

I'm reminded of the H. P. Lovecraft story "The Call of Cthulhu," in which a god sleeping beneath the ocean invades the dreams of humanity and, prior to his awakening, compels them to use new words and celebrate his image. Not because I worry we will soon be terrorized by a giant Mickey Mouse with tentacles, but because of the famous line "That is not dead which can eternal lie, and in strange aeons even death may die."

Disney's *Alien* franchise is about humanity. In all four of its mainline canonical films (*Alien*, *Aliens*, *Alien 3*, and *Alien: Resurrection*), protagonists try to not be hijacked by a non-human entity for purposes that work against their species. This is the surface of the text. The aliens procreate parasitically, using human bodies as incubators. A motif in the franchise is seeing a human become impregnated with a chest-burster and, not wanting to pay it forward, begging for death by rasping, "Kill me," before being euthanized in a flurry of bullets and flame.

But the xenomorphs are just a physical manifestation of the monolithic non-human entity at the heart of the series' conflict: the Weyland-Yutani Corporation. Whenever human-on-human violence occurs in *Alien* movies, it's between those acting sincerely on behalf of humanity and those on the payroll of an enterprise whose interests run counter to those of our species. At the end of each film, series hero Ellen Ripley defeats a xenomorph menace and is put into a preservative state in which she slumbers for decades. In each successive movie, when she is awoken from hypersleep or resurrected as a memory-retaining clone, the corporate ideology is still there. Even in *Alien: Resurrection*, set two hundred years after the events of *Alien 3*, in which Ripley self-immolated in front of a Weyland-Yutani executive, the company doesn't exist in name, but a government has taken up the anti-human torch, acting in the exact same meta-malicious way.

As futile as Ripley's generation-spanning quest seems, the *Alien* movies are optimistic. They are about confronting the invisible entities that manipulate us through greed and destroying their most toxic assets. Ripley literally dies trying to keep xenomorphs out of the hands of an industrial monstrosity, and as of 1997, when she last appeared onscreen, she looks to have succeeded. It's a beautiful thought, to imagine human camaraderie triumphing over the invisible tendrils of corporate greed. But when that message itself is a vector of a real industrial being that invades my dreams, it undercuts the hope.

Toppling our multinational overlords with teamwork and a flame-thrower taped to a grenade launcher is an inspirational idea. I want to rally behind the image of Ripley in a robotic exosuit, confronting the alien queen grasping for Newt, her surrogate daughter. But even that thought belongs to Disney. The anti-company champion I look to for hope of liberation is part of the same media product portfolio that abuses me in my sleep. Like Ripley, I want to stare the enemy in its toothy face and spit, "Get away from her, you bitch," on behalf of future generations who will also suffer invasive corporate nightmares. But it's too late for me—my brain's compromised; even my dreams of freedom are on the company dime.

THE NEW NECRONOMICON

Once upon a time, there was a little boy who, given access to his grandfather's library, read the entirety of *Grimm's Fairy Tales* and *Arabian Nights*. Obsessed with fantastical stories and high on his literary accomplishment, the boy refurbished his bedroom to reflect his fascination—trinkets and bobbles and curiosities that evoke images of distant lands—and he took a new name signifying his enlightenment. He read everything, so he called himself Alhazred (all-has-read) and he went on to pen a truly inaccessible book by virtue of its non-existence: *The Necronomicon*.

The Necronomicon is arguably the most famous imaginary book of the twentieth century. Literally translated as the "Book of Dead Names," it's said to contain Abdul Alhazred's prose descriptions of the ancient rites invoked to interact with a pantheon of transdimensional alien beings who once ruled over Earth and the cosmos. The information contained therein can, if applied, unleash unspeakable cosmic horrors on humanity. Bestial gods birthed by human wombs, weird messiahs, colours that kill, and tentacles, tentacles, tentacles. We should all be grateful that, despite goofy claims of its existence, such a terrible grimoire is just an imaginary book invented by H. P. Lovecraft—the real little boy who read his grandfather's books.

Lovecraft isn't just influential, he's an adjective for an entire sub-genre of horror. Lovecraftian: synonymous with secular, cosmic, pessimistic, misanthropic science fiction in which madness is enlightenment and to catch even a glimpse of the true nature of the universe is to know you're better off dead. "The Call of Cthulhu," *At the Mountains of Madness*, and "The Dunwich Horror" are the most famous among his catalogue of canonical stories exploring the darkest depths of that insignificant feeling you get when you look up at a clear night sky. But for all his foundational contributions to the horror genre, H. P. Lovecraft was an atrocious human being.

The pages of any given volume of Lovecraft's fiction, essays, or correspondence contain real hatred and prejudice, born of his deep-rooted white supremacy. Casual slurs abound, and in some instances, the dehumanization of non-white characters in his stories is so extreme that some apologetic academics claim Lovecraft is describing alien monsters rather than people. As a naive young reader myself, I misread his description of the eldritch apocalypse described in the prose poem "Nyarlathotep" as involving myriad yellow aliens from beyond the stars, when in fact he was expressing immigration anxiety in prose so purple it was nearly indistinguishable from fantasy. Other times, his depictions of African-American culture were upsetting even to my guileless eyes. Whether he was fetishizing Black communities in "The Call of Cthulhu," comparing an African-American security guard to a gorilla in "Herbert West—Reanimator," or affectionately naming a pet cat the N-word in "The Rats in the Walls," it was clear to me even at my most twentysomething-white-undergrad that Lovecraft was a racist beyond the conventional apologetics applied to classic literature.

The conflict between Lovecraft's politics and his fantasy is the subject of intense shame and denial. Many fans seem to worry his century-dead prejudice will stick to them if they admit to liking his writing. Some readers subscribe to the views put forward in the 2008 documentary *Lovecraft: Fear of the Unknown* that the author's racist leanings (which were prejudiced enough to spark debate with his weird fiction contemporaries like J. Vernon Shea) constitute an historical artifact rather than a living, breathing vector of oppression. Other defenders point to the widely accepted belief that Lovecraft's hate was equal-opportunity misanthropy. And while it's fair to say the old dead racist did hate all of humanity (*especially* Republicans) and has been credited with advancing the language and discourse of pessimism and cosmic nihilism, it's clearly evident in his work that even omniscient cosmic beings with complete disregard for humanity adhered to incorrect readings of Darwin. To Lovecraft, we're all worthless, but some of us are more worthless than others.

Want proof? Read miserable old Howard's "Beyond the Wall of Sleep," a short story notable for introducing sci-fi tropes still regularly used today, but also a story that's transformed into an utter joke by a cosmic being's monologue about human evolutionary hierarchies. First published by amateur literary journal *Pine Cones* in 1919, the story is the first-person account of an asylum intern who encounters a patient named Joe Slater. A wild man hailing from New York's Catskill Mountains, Slater was admitted after killing his neighbour in a jabbering fit of telepathic possession from beyond the stars. The mountain man, it turns out, is the corporeal prison to which a space-borne entity of light is bound, and in taking possession of Slater it communicates to the intern the true nature of existence: dreams comprise the prime plane of experience and human waking life is a mere facsimile of true reality. It's exactly the kind of pop-philosophy-turned-dark that made Lovecraft a founding master of the horror genre. The story is brought to life with over-the-top prose and beautiful imagery—and then the monologue happens.

The intern attempts to communicate directly with the entity inside Slater, using a machine intended for telepathic connection. He transcends his human body, sees the true dreamland nature of reality, and speaks to the imprisoned being of light. It's here we learn of the star-thing's politics on human bloodlines. Of Slater, the being says: "He was too much of an animal, too little a man; yet it is through his deficiency that you have come to discover me..."

That's right: Lovecraft writes that a cosmic entity believes in a hierarchy of human sophistication in line with the kind of bad science that empowers the most hateful and self-destructive behaviours of which our species is capable. A Lovecraft apologist could argue that any such eugenical beliefs held by the intern are a product of the era, but the star-bigot's monologue is an embarrassing piece of text that undercuts the story's main theme of all-too-human pessimism. If the takeaway is supposed to be that humans are insignificant in the face of the universe's true nature, then the puffing of an asylum worker's ego is fully contradictory: humans are insignificant, but their arbitrary self-categorization has merit in the minds of indifferent gods.

This type of thematic hypocrisy is throughout Lovecraft's fiction, but "Beyond the Wall of Sleep" is notable because it illustrates the gross extent of his bigotry. Slater is a white American man from an invented mountain community, and the author uses his ideas of lineage to dehumanize the guy. It's racial hatred of the most meticulous tier.

The literary genre community started revising Lovecraft's status as horror's mascot in 2015, which was the last year his weird likeness was used as a trophy for the World Fantasy Awards. A petition immediately began circulating to have the Lovecraft bust replaced with one of Octavia Butler, the African-American sci-fi and horror author responsible for bolstering the vampire canon with her novel *Fledgling*. The decision to change the award received pushback from the usual angry Internet suspects but was roundly and rightly championed by the most exciting genre fiction creators writing today. Genre, after all, is a tool of subversion, and to have an award for excellence in sci-fi, fantasy, and horror modelled as the likeness of an oppressive man's face is ironic in the worst way. In 2016, Lovecraft's bust was replaced with the sculpture of a twisted tree in front of a full moon.

The replacement of Lovecraft's statuette initiated a wave of aggressive canonical revisionism within the Internet horror fandom community. Even Joseph Fink, creator of the immensely popular Lovecraftian horror comedy podcast *Welcome to Nightvale,* added his stone to the pile. "He is a bad writer and, I think, a bad person," said Fink in an interview with Ed Power for the *Irish Times*. "There have been other writers who have done more with the same ideas. They don't get the same credit. I'm kind of tired with the attention he enjoys."

Fink's assessment is an increasingly popular opinion. Yet, we can't fully divest of Lovecraft because his spectre haunts all modern horror fiction and because dismissing Lovecraft's work outright ignores its most important aspect: it belongs to us. The imagery, the concepts, the tentacles— everything that's come to symbolize Providence, Rhode Island's most controversial export—it's all the property of horror fans of every race, gender, orientation, and, well, probably not creed because no matter how you slice it, Cthulhu and company are high blasphemy.

And it was this way from the beginning. Lovecraft isn't necessarily popular because he was a good writer, but because he was an enthusiastic collaborator who fostered an open-access philosophy, exemplified by the Lovecraft

Circle: a group of his friends and fans who contributed to many of the horror staples commonly attributed solely to H.P. himself. Take the so-called Cthulhu Mythos, which is generally what people think of when they hear Lovecraft's name; he had very little to do with its development.

The term "Cthulhu Mythos" was coined by Circle member August Derleth after Lovecraft's death. Derleth claimed to be a co-author with Lovecraft on over a dozen posthumously published stories, but the truth is he wrote his own tales around brief fragments the dead man left behind. These stories are not nearly as celebrated Lovecraft's Arkham Cycle (which contains his most famous eldritch icons), but they are arguably just as important to upholding the cultural image of the Lovecraftian sub-genre. After all, we are introduced to Lovecraft in Mythos-first fashion. We likely don't read "The Call of Cthulhu" right away. We see allusions to the titular god-monster in another story, like Neil Gaiman's "A Study in Emerald," or Guillermo Del Toro's film adaptation of *Hellboy*, or in a Metallica song, and then we work our way back. We see Season 1 of *True Detective*, read a review online, and find ourselves reading *The King in Yellow* by Robert W. Chambers, which is counted among the Mythos by virtue of Lovecraft's references to it in his fiction.

We see a system of connections emerge, and in a curious quest to know the divine underpinnings of disparate fiction titles, we read on, just like little all-has-reads. Because no one owns the pantheon of unspeakable gods and the trans-dimensional planes they inhabit, the creatives among us incorporate them into their fiction, or revisionist literature like Matt Ruff's *Lovecraft Country* and Silvia Moreno-Garcia's *Mexican Gothic..* Or tabletop role-playing games and shows like *Stranger Things*. Perhaps most powerfully, the Mythos is transplanted into video games.

The same year Lovecraft was dismissed as the mascot for the World Fantasy Awards, two notable video games that borrow from his tradition were released: *Sunless Sea*, a Lovecraftian game of exploration from Failbetter Games that has characters navigate an underground ocean on a steam-powered ship, and *Bloodborne*, a game developed by From Software in which players must confront the deepest human evils that emerge when divine knowledge is exploited before it's understood. Both games have all the hallmarks and symbols of the Lovecraftian tradition but none of the bigotry. They understand by design that the mythology is equally accessible by all, and therefore each game begins with a character-creation option, allowing the player to customize their likeness. *Sunless Sea* even lets you choose your character's pronoun.

With an open-door attitude toward their mythologies, *Bloodborne* and *Sunless Sea* explore themes that have always been Lovecraft hooks, but they do so with true equal-opportunity nihilism. There are no omniscient racists spouting monologues on the virtues of bad science; there are no lazily drawn enemies that exploit assumed xenophobia in the reader. You can come to these games as you are, or even as you wish to be, and experience the horror just like anyone else.

By reimagining Lovecraft in an inclusive way, Failbetter Games and From Software achieved what the racist always attempted but never published. In an oft-quoted 1927 letter to Farnsworth Wright, the editor of *Weird Tales* magazine, Lovecraft summed up his literary aspirations succinctly: he wanted to create tales that negate the human. In practice, his white supremacy undermined his intention, because if we are all nothing, then we must also all be equal. Now, with *Sunless Sea*, *Bloodborne*, and the countless other

Lovecraft-revisionist games, we see his successors proving his worst opinions wrong while using his own creations. Fans, audiences, and creators aren't apologizing anymore; they're delving into the forbidden texts, appropriating their imagery, and truly gazing into the void.

We must always read until we can say all has been read, including the unreadable. The most dreadful books of old contain horrors, but it's only through facing those horrors that we can understand how to contain them, lest we make the same mistakes. The only knowledge that can truly harm us is the knowledge we ignore.

THE SHATTERED TEACUP

Garret Jacob Hobbs was eating people. That was FBI special agent Will Graham's conclusion. Hobbs, known in the tabloids as the Minnesota Shrike, identified women bearing a strong likeness to his daughter, Abigail—young, brown hair, wind-chafed skin—and proceeded to hunt them like deer. Garret "honoured" his victims by using every part of their corpses. What he didn't eat, he used as crafting materials. Will, working with the FBI's Behavioral Science Unit, tracked the cannibal down and, finding him in the Hobbs family kitchen, shot him to death—but not before the Shrike killed his wife and sliced open an artery in Abigail's throat.

The immediate aftermath is a scene of nightmares: a suburban American home covered in blood spatter. Prone bodies, one dead, two dying, and a shell-shocked, bespectacled gunman standing over them. Garret Jacob Hobbs staring into Will Graham's eyes and, with his last breath, repeating the word "See?"

Will's partner, his FBI-appointed psychiatrist Hannibal Lecter, saves Abigail. He places his calm hand over the spurting wound on the girl's neck and rides with her in the ambulance to a hospital.

This massacre is the inciting incident of NBC's *Hannibal*, a television adaptation of Thomas Harris's Hannibal Lecter novels, primarily *Red Dragon*. It's a crime procedural presented through the lens of horror, and it deals with the irreversible, transformative effects of extreme traumatic violence. The execution of Garret Jacob Hobbs represents the breaching of an existential boundary for Will, and as the series progresses he attempts to understand, through therapy, how killing another human being positions him in the larger ethical framework of society. The show's hook is that Will's psychiatrist is none other than the most infamous literary cannibal since the Greek god Cronus.

Hannibal Lecter is an enduring monster who has inspired fear, fascination, and fandom for decades, across four novels—*Red Dragon*, *Silence of the Lambs*, *Hannibal*, and *Hannibal Rising*—and their film and television adaptations. The character has undergone metamorphoses, from the creepy little Lithuanian on the page, to Brian Cox's dangerous mind in a cell, the iconic skeez of Anthony Hopkins, the forgettable emo chic of Gaspard Ulliel, and finally the sublime apex predator that is Mads Mikkelsen's portrayal on the show. Hannibal topped the American Film Institute's 2003 list of the hundred greatest villains, beating out Norman Bates, Darth Vader, and the Wicked Witch of the West. He's always the smartest person in any universe that contains him, almost supernaturally gifted with good taste in art and cuisine, and he can't get enough of Glenn Gould's rendition of Bach's *Goldberg Variations*. He eats humans, he's foreign, devious, and dangerous, he hates God—short of committing vampirism, Hannibal Lecter is practically Dracula all over again.

But no one ever talks about all the good Hannibal Lecter does. He's not an anti-hero serial killer in the vein of Dexter from *Dexter*, who channels his badness to serve the greater good while breaking the law; Hannibal represents the embodiment of true omnipotent evil, doing good by granting gnosis to the traumatized. And of all his patients who have received his dark enlightenment, it's Will Graham from the television show who best illustrates why we need a big bad cannibal psychiatrist: Hannibal Lecter liberates us from the oppression of normative, naive society.

When you're traumatized, everything normal seems like a deception. The moment of violence that causes trauma is unpleasant, but in my experience the worst agony comes during the aftermath. Everyday life and its quotidian worries seem insignificant when compared to the moment of trauma, which seems so hyper-real as to inspire obsession. After trauma, safety looks like a cheap illusion, and people who feel safe appear naive for not having also realized that catastrophe can visit at any moment. It's like achieving enlightenment for an adrenaline-soaked day, hour, minute, or second, then being sucked back into Plato's Cave, where no one understands the concept of the "sunlight" you keep raving about.

I'm not in law enforcement, but I do have post-traumatic stress disorder, and I can relate to Will Graham. When I was nineteen, my parents took me on a Christmas cruise vacation, and during a stop in a small Costa Rican town my father and I were approached by a man who attempted to rob us at gunpoint, realized we weren't carrying anything of value, shot my dad in the chest, and fled down a nearby alleyway. I had to carry the bleeding body of my two-hundred-pound father from the wooden pier where he was shot back to our ship, falling a bunch of times, screaming for help, getting covered in his blood.

Dad survived, thanks to the actions of the ship's medical officer who'd treated gunshot wounds in South Africa, and by the end of the day our cruise vacation continued. The worst experience of my life was followed by four more days of booze-soaked floating casino resort luxury, encouraging me to adopt the apathy of my fellow cruisers, the ship's crew, and even my family. My mom and brother didn't learn about the shooting until I broke down crying at our table in the dining hall, and even then, the whole ordeal must have seemed too abstract to scar them in the same way it scrambled my brain. When the cruise was over, I went back to theatre school, where I encountered the same indifference from friends and mentors. Life continued as normal. Everyone ignored the existential lesson I'd carried back like a grim souvenir: that in the face of mortal violence, all else is inconsequential. It should surprise no one that I needed therapy to recover.

Even today, over a decade after that screaming, bloody morning in Costa Rica, people don't want to hear me reference it. The idea that violence could puncture something so ordered and wholesome as a family vacation stands in defiance of the base comfort we expect from life. So unless I'm feeling sanctimonious on Twitter, or I'm especially broody and drunk, I've learned to just shut up about it. Which is painful, because for me it was a moment of revelation, and I'm tacitly asked to treat it like a bad dream.

That bad dream state is the ambience of *Hannibal*. Will Graham becomes obsessed with the murder of Garret Jacob Hobbs, the first violation of his world's order. Over the subsequent thirty-five episodes, Will goes on a cognitive behavioural journey to accept how violence has transformed him. From the initial days in which he begins to confuse his identity with that of Garret, becoming a surrogate father figure to Abigail, to his flirtation with lawlessness in a bid to reassert order and symbolically erase his trauma, through to the series conclusion when he finally learns to accept a world in which trauma is truth, Will's journey mirrors the PTSD survival experience. Forced into a state of chaos in the Hobbs kitchen, an irreversible act of violence causes a state of revelation, he fights back in a futile attempt to assert control over the unchangeable past, and finally comes to accept himself as divergent. (It's worth stating here that engaging in cannibalism is not a phase in the recovery process for PTSD.)

Hannibal Lecter is a trauma normalizer, and we understand this romantically. He is not like the other deranged minds locked up in Frederick Chilton's hospital for the criminally insane. He offers truth and self-knowing in all their dangerous, liberating glory. His relationship with Clarice Starling in *The Silence of the Lambs* was the cultural entry point to this concept. In both the film and the novel, Lecter is not a villain but rather a dangerous sounding board for the young Clarice as she attempts to understand the mind of the serial killer Buffalo Bill. Lecter is presented as dangerous, but also hyperaware of reality's true chaotic nature, which is not the reality of American law enforcement. When he first meets Clarice, he practically smells her own past trauma, and in their subsequent visits he essentially takes her through a therapeutic process, aiding her in knowing herself and combatting the elemental monstrosity that is the male gaze incarnate.

Clarice's revelation and rehabilitation from her traumatic childhood takes on a romantic air, because her moments with Hannibal are the only ones in which she is allowed to acknowledge the bad dream state of the world, with its unspoken horrors that are swept under the rug by institution, social order, and law. *Hannibal* the novel, the sequel to *The Silence of the Lambs*, further develops this romance, to the point where Clarice is shown the liberation of being Dr. Lecter's equal. She forsakes law enforcement, accepts the nature of the world, and partakes in cannibalism.

Clarice Starling never made it into NBC's *Hannibal*, but the televised version of Will Graham contains a significant amount of her narrative DNA. Over the course of the show, Will's relationship with Hannibal also displays a romantic heat, one that's led an active fandom to believe there's evidence the men have an off-screen sexual relationship. That romantic tension, however you wish to read it, is the longing for a wounded outsider to be understood. Will Graham and Clarice Starling both want the same thing: they want to be normal. Hannibal Lecter's gift to them is denying what they want on principle, saying that the source of their pain and confusion is that they're right and the normative world is wrong.

The format of NBC's *Hannibal* illustrates the oppressive nature of law and society on the neurodivergent outsider. Its crime procedural format is subverted by the pessimistic philosophy of horror. Established over a century ago by Arthur Conan Doyle's Sherlock Holmes stories, the procedural proliferated throughout mainstream entertainment and eventually became the de facto vehicle for the law enforcement authority porn of myriad *CSI* and *Law & Order* television shows. The modern crime procedural is social order in motion. Well-known characters who work for the state employ critical thinking, deduction, and technology to ensure a criminal of the week is either put behind bars or righteously murdered in the name of the law.

It's all delivered expectation—a murder gives way to a familiar title sequence and twenty-five minutes of guest stars being interviewed, the occasional gunfight, foot chase, or clever infiltration, and finally a conclusion that results in justice. As a final narrative button, procedural episodes often have a short epilogue involving the series regulars to underline their humanity, their ongoing struggle to maintain order, and the belief in inherent safety. The good guys win because they're the good guys.

Hannibal flips the script on the procedural's institutional optimism, following its plot structure while constantly breaking to empathize with the killers. When not commenting directly on the grisly affairs that anchor each individual episode, Will and Hannibal's therapy sessions often run thematically parallel to the case of the week. Lecter's motivation is getting Will to a point where he can understand how he's shackled by the rule of law. But getting inside the heads of guest-star murderers is a slippery slope, and each episode's final emotional beats hammer down on the sorrowful and contemplative. Aren't we all trying to find a deeper connection to the divine, just like the guy sewing the bodies of his victims into a fleshy mandala that looks like the giant eyeball of God?

My therapist is not a cannibal. Middle-aged and grey-haired, he worked out of his condo in downtown Toronto. He had back problems. On my first day in his office, he asked what I wanted to accomplish during my time with him. I said I wanted things to be normal again, like they were before I'd felt the texture of my dad's blood and heard the real sound of a gunshot. The two interceding years were unsettling when they weren't tortuous. Everything—socializing, school, my job at the chocolate store in the mall—was in defiance of what I knew to be the real nature of the world: violence, chaos, lingering adrenaline. In comparison to dragging a bleeding body through foreign streets, everyday life felt dull, and that terrified me. Whatever I did was doomed to comparison with gun violence and the terrifying importance of life-or-death stakes.

My therapist laughed. No one could return my life to its pre-traumatic state because I was sick with an event, not a virus. To try and fix the lasting effects of trauma in the same way we treat skin blemishes or minor illnesses is not only dishonest, it's the equivalent of a lobotomy. It's clinical digression achieved through further violence.

In therapy I learned my post-traumatic feelings weren't wrong. My reality wasn't forfeit just because people didn't want to acknowledge it. Afterward, I was initiated into the ranks of the healthy neurodivergent. And four years later, *Hannibal* premiered on TV, presenting an expressionist narrative that further validated my honest, if alienating, recovery.

In the final scenes of a brutal Season 2 finale, during which Hannibal Lecter reveals his true identity and leaves every main character half-butchered and dying as he escapes to Europe, the post-traumatic ferryman recites a monologue from deep within his character's literary history. He talks about a dropped teacup, and how, when looking at its shards on the ground, he grows frustrated and wants the laws of cause and effect to reverse so the teacup might come back together. He then reopens the wound on Abigail Hobbs's throat, the one he'd initially covered with his hand during that first episode, and lets entropy take its course.

With the essential Hannibal in plain view, Will is challenged to accept a world without order. The remainder of the series is fully serialized rather than episodic, no longer held in place by the week-to-week familiarity of law in motion. It depicts a shattered-teacup world in which honesty and connection supercede normativity and comfort. It's Hannibal Lecter's gift to the horrifically enlightened. It's the realization of impact, survival, and the assurance that trauma opens new ways of knowing.

We learn tasseomancy to read our teacup lives, interpreting meaning from the sediments of our daily experience. That morning in Costa Rica, when I saw my father crumple from contact with a bullet, my teacup broke into countless shards. To continue on, I had to learn a new way of comprehending life. I stared at the pieces on the ground, frustrated like Hannibal Lecter, and began to divine their meaning instead. I read the sharp objects now.

ON THE HORROR OF COMEDY

Alone in his sibling's condo, Niles, the persnickety younger brother of Seattle radio therapist Frasier Crane, is being tortured for entertainment. Cooking dinner for a Valentine's date with only a Jack Russell terrier named Eddie for company, Niles notices the crease in his trousers is misaligned, so he removes them. While ironing, the pantsless Crane then finds a loose thread and, trimming it with scissors retrieved from the kitchen, snips his finger. The sight of the wound makes Niles faint onto the couch, the hot iron still face down on his pants. The walls laugh.

Frasier was filmed in front of a live studio audience. About 250 human beings sat in risers just beyond the reality of Niles's crisis, peering through the fourth wall, expecting to be entertained and laughing when prompted. Their reactions are etched into that moment of the younger Dr. Crane's life, imprinting it with a weird humiliation he was at least vaguely aware of, pausing in action to let the cackling finish before making his next inevitable mistake. The show was broadcast and recorded, and replayed ad nauseum on syndicated television and streaming services, trapping Niles Crane in a six-minute loop of eternal peril, like Sisyphus with a failed date instead of a boulder. But Niles doesn't know that. He doesn't know that the roars of amusement at his misfortune are anything but a terrible, mocking environmental force. All he wants is to make a good impression on a romantic interest. But we know he is doomed.

Eddie the dog wakes poor half-naked Niles from unconsciousness. But now there's blood on the sofa. Niles uses turpentine to remove the red stain, sees his mutilated finger in the process, and passes out a second time. He spills the flammable liquid, drenching one of the seat cushions. Eddie barks, rousing Niles again, who promptly checks on the food in the kitchen. Noticing a burning smell, he follows his nose back to the living room to find his slacks ablaze on the ironing board. He tries to smother the flame, burns himself, and tosses the pants onto the couch, which ignites. The walls laugh louder.

High stakes are essential in comedy. The subjects of our laughter need to care as if their continued existence depends on taking the present moment seriously. That is, after all, how life is lived. Against prior conditioning, we allow ourselves to hope, and we set expectations, however fated they might be to fall away in the face of surprise and disaster. We love to laugh at Niles Crane as he's on the verge of living cremation because we anticipate the failure he is incapable of forecasting. We know the rules governing his life. We know what it's like to be him, overtaken by an ingrained compulsion.

To flail about as our world collapses according to a script would be terrible, a nightmarish farce with jumpscares instead of jokes. But people laugh at horror movies too. We laugh watching a fountain of blood erupt from the bed that eats Johnny Depp in *A Nightmare on Elm Street*. We laugh at the suicidal cliff jump that turns a cultist's face to pulp on the first day of *Midsommar's* terrible solstice party. We laugh as Pennywise the dancing clown grows a set of jagged shark teeth and bites the arm off a small child in *It*. We laugh to prove the pain onscreen isn't our own. We are safe.

Treading water in an ocean of roaring, invisible strangers hooting and cackling and gasping for air, Niles retrieves a fire extinguisher and sprays white flame retardant on everything but the burning cushions. It's as if some cruel force has engineered his failure. In a desperate attempt to save the condo, he retrieves the pots of boiling food from the stove and douses the flames. He opens the door to air out the suffocating smoke, but upon seeing the brutal lesion on his finger, he faints a final time. Spread-eagled under black clouds, the semi-nude Niles Crane lies unconscious as the fire alarm finally starts to scream.

The walls laugh louder and louder.

MANUFACTURING MEPHISTOPHELES

The Husqvarna 460 Rancher gas-powered chainsaw is a monster. It features a twenty-four-inch steel bar, three-piece crankshaft ensuring maximum durability, and an angled front handle to allow for ideal grip position. Proprietary Smart Start® technology guarantees you'll never have trouble on start-up, and its two-cycle, 60 cc engine is optimized for reliable performance. It's both eco-friendly and easy to maintain. No power cord means no tripping hazards and unlimited range. Rip and roar!

The chainsaw has an orange plastic body that screams heavy-duty, and the chain hugging its steel bar (what one might colloquially call the saw blade) looks like the mouth of an angry shark turned inside out and galvanized. It's a thing of utility, but also luxury. The brand name is displayed on the steel bar and body with pride. If I fell on this thirteen-pound lumber maker and its automatic oiling system while it was buzzing, I'd be able to read the name of the lifeless metal assemblage mutilating me, even if I might still be trying to work out its phonetic pronunciation as my vision faded to black. Husqvarna ("hoosk-vaa-nah"): a city in southern Sweden, home to an eponymous musket manufacturer founded in 1689 that now makes various outdoor power products like chainsaws.

Sitting unpowered, the chainsaw is an unthinking, unmoving assemblage of carbon and metal, oil and plastic and potential motion. But pull the recoil starter rope and you summon a demon. Sure, the Husqvarna 460 Rancher gas chainsaw is intended for the efficient deconstruction of timber, but its blade is indifferent to what it cuts. It will spin and spin until it runs out of fuel. This is the kind of tool Patrick Bateman swings wildly in front of his nearly nude body as he chases a sex worker through the halls of his condo building in *American Psycho*—a hand-held black hole he practically rides like a bull until he comes to the edge of the stairwell down which his victim is attempting to escape. Bateman dangles the whirring machine in open air before simply letting go, allowing it to do what it does naturally: masticate, lacerate—as it descends multiple storeys onto the woman below.

It's secular magic. Animated by the pull of a rope, a chainsaw is machinery possessed, demonic in that it is at once dead and moving. Ancient fossil fuels reawakened in a cacophony of engine noise and exhaust fumes, a chainsaw is benign nature repurposed and activated. It's practically divine.

There's no rule that says ghosts can't use power tools or psycho killers can't also be vampires. And yet there's a whole sub-genre dedicated to humans torturing other humans without a pentagram in sight. Extreme horror: the *Hostels* and *Saws* and *Texas Chain Saw Massacres* of the world are gruesome stories that, if not already loosely based on true events, could conceivably be recreated by just about anyone with enough time, money, and hate-fuelled trips to Home Depot. Brutal and visceral, extreme horror is almost terminally uncreative, foregoing interesting ideas about the nature of existence in favour of the exploitation of pain or, worse, vicarious sadism. It's C-minus horror, satisfactory but uninspired, tactile but dumb. Extreme horror is scary stories jocks tell in the dark. And yet it still frightens me.

If that assessment seems defensive or catty, it's because my desire for more spookiness in my torture porn is a fear reaction. The old gods and poltergeists and cosmic terrors of supernatural horror add a layer of existential surprise to human suffering that makes the pain more palatable, creating an intellectual distance and turning the fear into fun. Getting disembowelled by a skinhead's pit bull is just an unlucky period at the end of your personal story's last sentence, but having your intestines ripped out by a werewolf is an entertaining twist in life's final lines. *Wow*, you might think as the beast works its muzzle into a gash in your belly. *I've witnessed a lot of things in my time on this planet but I never expected to see a werewolf.*

While extreme horror and supernatural horror seem to be at odds, they aren't polar opposites. Both sub-genres do the same thing: they bring humans in contact with the anti-human. Our insignificance as people is the nuclear core that holds all horror together, and that core is made manifest by independent non-human annihilators. For the supernatural, these annihilators are metaphysical anomalies that require a fantastical imagination, scary monsters, and weird phenomena that defy natural law. In extreme horror, easy-to-imagine technology stands in for the transdimensional tentacle beasts and haunted dolls, bringing the threat closer to our reality. It's tempting to blame all the suffering on the Leatherfaces and insane sadists—the hillbillies and superfreaks living outside the bounds of civilization—but the chainsaw is the vector of annihilation, not the maniac wielding it. The machine holders are as subject to its optimized torque as you are— they're just not in its deadly path.

Technology in general is a secularizing force. Hippies in the 1960s, rejecting the Christian Church of the establishment, replaced God with the psychedelic experience enabled by LSD. Chemical technology engineered an atheistic spiritual revelation that could be bought and sold. Lacking the language to describe the ways of thinking unlocked by acid, baby boomers turned to mysticism and other religions to navigate their new world view. Psychedelia looks like spirituality and sounds like spirituality, but it's just chemistry.

The acid experience can be used to help understand the relationship between supernatural horror and extreme horror in much the same way. Panos Cosmatos's 2018 splatterfest *Mandy* is extreme horror presented through the lens of dark psychedelia to such an extent that it reads as nearly supernatural. The film follows Mandy and Red, an outsider couple played by Andrea Riseborough and Nic Cage. The two are abducted by a group of tripped-out Jesus freaks organized under the name Children of the New Dawn, and when Mandy ridicules the cult's leader for his pathetic sexual advances, the sect burns her to death in front of a bound and sober Red.

The remainder of the film is a study in revenge, evisceration, and lucidity. Fuelled by adrenaline, vodka, cocaine, and the same bad acid the Children of the New Dawn use, Red's emotional journey from hypersensitivity to permanent psychedelia is represented through dynamic frame rate changes, colour, and contrast. His most lucid moment—a career-topping scene for Cage in which he cries and screams and laughs in white underpants and a T-shirt while chugging a bottle of vodka—is under harsh white light without a lens filter, giving it a home-video hyperrealistic feel. LSD scenes, on the other hand, are bathed in coloured light and contain imagery so absurd that it brings into question the reliability of the camera as a narrator.

It's as if psychedelic drugs unlock new ways of knowing physical existence, and in representing this amorphous yet secular world, *Mandy* decentralizes the sober human experience as the defining factor of reality. Technology dislodges us, makes us insignificant, strips our gaze of its authority over the definition of conscious existence. And when we accept we have no control over reality, the demarcation between supernatural and natural is practically incomprehensible. It's just a matter of the language we use to describe the things that scare us.

In extreme horror, the use of technology is a stand-in for occult summoning. It's the interface between the human and the non-human. LSD unlocks ways of knowing in *Mandy*, but it's manufactured tools that open the portal to annihilation. In preparing for his rampage, Red melts down metal ore to create an elegant silver axe, transfiguring the natural world to serve his bloody purpose. In the film's rising action, technology becomes climatological when Nic Cage and one of the Jesus freaks have a chainsaw fight that ends with the cultist falling onto the spinning blade of a still-active machine with a comically huge steel bar. Pulling the starter rope on a chainsaw is setting natural obliterating forces in motion. Like summoning a tiny metal hurricane, starting a chainsaw is an elemental act.

Technology is also a bridge to the supernatural. Humans learn the arcane secrets of natural law and use them to create the anti-human, which can be indistinguishable from the paranormal. This is especially true when human ingenuity intersects with the atomic.

Consider the demon core, a 6.2 kilogram spherical mass of plutonium, coated with nickel to prevent corrosion, intended for use in World War II but left undetonated in the wake of Japan's surrender four days prior to its scheduled bombing. Nicknamed Rufus, the core remained at the Los

Alamos Laboratory in New Mexico, where it was subjected to testing.

Since Rufus was designed as a weapon, it was configured to easily slip into supercriticality, the state of nuclear chain reaction that can lead to an explosion of mass destruction. It was an unstable manufactured piece of nature, an independent non-human annihilator that killed scientists during two tests to measure its volatility. In 1945, a physicist named Harry Daghlian was arranging neuron-reflective bricks around the plutonium and dropped one directly onto the core, nudging it into a chain reaction and irradiating himself and a security guard. Daghlian died twenty-five days later from radiation poisoning, and the guard, Robert J. Hemmerly, was killed by leukemia thirty-three years later. Nine months after Daghlian's lethal mishap, another test was conducted on Rufus, this time involving its containment in a neuron-reflective casing consisting of two beryllium semi-spheres. Canadian physicist Louis Alexander Slotin conducted the procedure against protocol, using the stem of a screwdriver to prevent the beryllium casing from closing completely. Slotin's hand slipped and a chain reaction occurred, bathing the physicist in a flash of radiation that caused his death nine days later. The mass was renamed the demon core, and all subsequent testing was performed remotely, at a distance of a quarter mile.

The demon core never exploded; it simply released radiation when disturbed. The phenomenon that led to the deaths of Rufus's testers was invisible. Gamma radiation is a wave, not a particle; you don't feel it, you can't see it, but when it passes through you it tears apart your molecules, which reform in incorrect configurations. The water that makes up ninety-nine percent of a human body, for instance, can fall apart at the atomic level and react with other pieces of busted-up H_2O to form hydrogen, oxygen, or hydrogen peroxide. Your DNA gets all mixed up, your cells no longer have the correct information to reproduce, and you essentially stop working. Your bone marrow halts the production of white blood cells, your digestive system ceases to absorb nutrients, your circulatory system floods like a broken engine, you get cancer. You either die right away or years later from the unnatural transformation brought about through proximity to something both indifferent and malevolent, a lethal force described by science but named for the supernatural.

The gamma radiation of the demon core does not occur naturally on Earth. It was unlocked in the same manner that Faustus brought forth Mephistopheles from beyond the pale. The places haunted by the spectre of nuclear fallout—disaster sites like Fukushima and Chernobyl, and the tomblike vaults where we lay atomic waste like cursed mummies—we made them anti-human, and the paradigm by which we understand that fact is trivial. Religion, literature, and spirituality give us the lexicon for supernatural horrors. History, science, and engineering help us understand extreme secular horrors. Chainsaws aren't all that different from demons. Werewolves and pit bulls, radiation and spell books—they all destroy us, no matter how we define them.

BEEPS AND BOOPS

Welcome to the Haunted Mansion: We passed the cat-shaped sign on our way to the Confederation Bridge. The building was a massive brown-and-white Tudor-style manor imposed on the blue sky above Kensington, Prince Edward Island. I did a double take. The island is full of surprises—everyone talks about the potatoes and the unbelievably red beaches and Green Gables, but never the fields of old roller coasters and midway rides that litter Cavendish. And never this haunted house.

"Want to go?" said Emma.

"Maybe next time." I was fixated on our travel itinerary. Emma, Nick, and I were heading to the Bay of Fundy. We did have the time to pull over for a few minutes, but sometimes my brain gets stuck in its Turingesque preset order of operations.

"If we don't go now, you know we'll never come back."

She was right. I pulled a U-turn and parked in the shadow of the mansion like some tourist version of Eleanor Vance from *The Haunting of Hill House*. We took a few pictures of the spooked-up bits of ornamentation, little silhouettes of bats that underlined the second storey, the one bay window bordered by gold insectine chimeras: beetles with dragons for mandibles and scorpions carved into their thoraxes. As we angled for the best view, one of the highest windows burst open. The shape of a limp woman in a gown threw herself halfway over the ledge and screamed for help, begging for release in an Islander's accent.

"Robots!" said Nick. And we knew we'd made the right choice in pulling over.

PEI's Haunted Mansion is perfect. They say it was built in the late nineteenth century by a man named Dr. Jack, who operated it as an inn. At least one suspected murder was committed within its walls, and Lizzy Borden allegedly signed its guest book. The mansion has since been retrofitted as a three-level maze of spooky dioramas and animatronic jumpscares. Admittance costs less than twenty bucks, and when you fork it over, the gothy woman with frizzy auburn hair at the ticket booth attaches a wristband listing your morgue admission info to your arm. Entrance into the house presumes death.

Emma, Nick, and I crept from room to room. We beheld a meticulously staged seance with old-fashioned stage effects that produced a holographic spectre floating above mannequins seated at a table. We saw a mad scientist torturing a pizza delivery guy. We witnessed a birthday cake made with human remains presented to a wise-cracking decapitated head. We even accidentally walked in on a monster using the toilet—it screamed in embarrassment and slammed the bathroom door on us. All of these sights were animated and wondrous and kitschy. All of them were robotic. The only humans we encountered were other travellers cautiously stalking the mansion, bracing themselves for the next bizarre sight or programmed surprise—and the woman in the gift shop at the exit, so closely resembling the ticket booth attendant we initially thought they were the same person.

If you look for them, you can see motion sensors as you tour the Haunted Mansion. The building sees you, feels you, and then reveals itself. Some shocks are simple, like an air cannon blasting your face as you turn a corner. Others are truly terrifying. The three of us settled into a rhythm, snaking through the halls in single file, reconfiguring our formation after every scream so someone new was in front. That's how I got a perfect view of the most terrifying image I've ever seen: a skeleton in a dress, wielding an axe and screaming as it burst forth from a portrait above a fireplace, bearing down on my partner and brother. The spasming axe swings felt truly violent, and Emma and Nick scurried across the otherwise cozy study in fear. As I entered, even though the trap had been sprung and no surprises remained in the room, I still recoiled under the violent persistence of the skeleton lady's forty clockwork whacks.

Every October, Canada's Wonderland holds Fright Fest, a Halloween event during which the amusement park supplements its roller coasters with haunted houses populated by contract-working theatre students and high schoolers in monster costumes. The low-level labyrinths are themed on horror clichés—the corn maze, the asylum—and each features its own flavour of fright.

In the hillbilly horror maze, as we walk through scarecrow-stuffed galleries of hay bales and cornstalks, the smell of gasoline accompanies the roar of defanged chainsaws swung wildly by hockey-masked murderous hicks. I'm compelled to run, not because the illusion that I will be torn apart by an off-brand Jason or Leatherface is so believable, but because if I don't play my role as frightened customer number 1,408, the illusion will be broken. Both me and my would-be murderer would have to acknowledge the strange transaction, the park employee stopping short, impotently swinging a power tool and screaming, incapable of going further because of our silent contract: no touching the paying customers.

Awkward.

Machines don't have that level of intimacy. They aren't present in the same way people are. Nor are they subject to our social codes. Even those possessed by hostile arti-ficial intelligence are just beeps and boops with guns and knives. When Arnold Schwarzenegger's T-800 Terminator pursues Linda Hamilton, trying to prevent her from giv-ing birth to the human resistance, she is alone, as alone as the silent protagonist of "Metalhead," the episode of *Black Mirror* about a woman pursued by killer MIT dog drones. Flesh-and-blood monsters are different. Pinhead was human once, and the tortures he visits on victims are part of an extreme physical relationship—he's there the whole time, with his Cenobite pals, tearing your soul apart. Even a killer Humboldt squid has a heart and a mind. It sleeps. It might even dream.

Those chainsaw-wielding teens at Canada's Wonderland go home at midnight, take off their makeup, brush their teeth, and crawl into bed, hoping against nightmares. They go to school the next day. They wonder if it's cooler to show up to class on Halloween in costume or in plain-clothes. They are part-time monsters, full-time people. But the robot ghost of Lizzy Borden, who attacked my family with an axe? It's still mounted above the fireplace, in that haunted house on the hill in Kensington, PEI. The Lizzybot waits without anticipation. It's simply *there*: all potential energy, no frailty, no doubt, no hesitation, just an appliance in a building designed for nothing but scaring.

MANIFEST DOOM

Eleven people died on Mount Everest in 2019, eight of them during their descent from the summit. To add the hill to their list of personal conquests, they had to stand in a line of other climbers that snaked around the top of the mountain, adding hours to the climb. Meanwhile, experts say that human-caused climate change is shortening the window of opportunity for a safe trip back to Everest's base. It's an ironic death, coming down from Everest, having asserted a type of token ownership over a worn-out frontier, lined up to participate in colonial tradition, only to be claimed by the sixty-million-year-old peak and then forgotten.

Land isn't ours. It was here before we were born, and it'll be here after we're gone. The thing is, we might be gone soon. It's not just Everest—everywhere is going to get hotter, stormier, more suffocating. Cities will submerge into rising oceans. Tornadoes and hurricanes will fling us around like paper dolls. The planet will shake us off and transform. It won't be monstrous because we'll all be dead, and monstrosity is contingent on human comparison. Instead, we'll succumb to our greatest enemy: the deathless pale blue dot we live on.

In Jeff VanderMeer's weird-fiction opus, *The Southern Reach Trilogy*, he makes our blue-dot environment misanthropic for the sake of horror. After smashing into a coastal section of America, an unknown alien influence begins to alter its surroundings. Dubbed Area X by the government, the affected ecosystem undergoes an uncanny metamorphosis. Team after team of human specialists are sent into

Area X's lush, overgrown interior to explore what was once mapped, invaders on their own planet. They transform, slowly, into other things: dolphins with eyes like ours, a warthog displaying a human face, trees that vaguely resemble people, and unearthly towering beasts.

VanderMeer turns a familiar landscape into an exotic place using only the tiniest bit of exaggeration. A screaming monster here, a human doppelgänger there, and a splash of toxicity is all it takes to make a national park villainous. Earth is already sufficiently adversarial to those of us who order our lives and culture and government in ways that are cloistered from the natural dangers of the planet. When that hostility is emphasized in horror, and land is made demonic, the lie that we're in charge is eaten alive. Acknowledgement of our dependence on the globe runs counter to colonial ideas of land ownership. We strive to ascend from animalia to another kingdom that's less subject to the consequences of our quest for perpetual comfort, and in doing so encounter the planet's immune system. Terroir is the most abominable fiend.

The Terror, Dan Simmons's horror-novel-turned-AMC television series, explores Earth's natural anti-colonial eco-system through historical fiction. Based on a real-life expedition to find the Northwest Passage, *The Terror* chronicles the fates of the *HMS Erebus* and *HMS Terror*, the most technologically advanced ships of their age, as they and their crew are devoured by the Arctic.

The crews of *Erebus* and *Terror* use English names for land masses they don't even know the shape of. Rather than arrive with humility, they dig in their prescriptive imperial heels, claim the region as their own, and meet their horrific, icy ends. After abandoning their vessels, the remaining crew go on to find death in what's now Nunavut. Many freeze, fall to scurvy, and die of starvation. The rest are mutilated on the ice by a giant preternatural polar bear called the Tuunbaq. Like Area X, the Tuunbaq is a supernatural expression of an antagonistic land. It differs from VanderMeer's evil environment, however, in having clear agency—it only kills white people, not the Netsilik Inuit characters. In the climax of the television adaptation, the villain Cornelius Hickey cuts out his own tongue as an offering to the Tuunbaq, only to be swallowed whole by the elemental beast. *The Terror* isn't some manifest-destiny ice Western. It's reverse invasion fiction: *Dracula*, but this time we're the vampires.

Horror's climatological nature makes it a tool for anti-colonial resistance. Area X and the Tuunbaq are avatars of a raging planet, but resistance literature doesn't have to be so explicitly elemental. In Jeff Barnaby's zombie apocalypse film *Blood Quantum*, a zombifying pathogen does the trick. The Z virus in *Blood Quantum* only affects settlers, not the Mi'kmaq who weather the undead end of the world while hosting non-Indigenous refugees. Through the visceral genre language of chainsaw eviscerations, katana beheadings, and bitten-off genitals, Barnaby flips the table on the historical account of ongoing genocide in Canada, stripping settlers of privilege and subjecting them to a narrative-justified environmental annihilation. But beyond that surface reading, there's a deeper, more nuanced thread about the relationship between space and ownership. The settlers have always been hostile to Indigenous populations, invaders moving with impunity in great waves and wreaking havoc. There's practically no difference between imperialists and zombies. We are the apocalypse.

The world isn't ending. The world is fine. It's humans that are fucked. The world is just rock and water and air with a bunch of carbon covering it that makes things move. Like one of those bad stars or deathless gods from cosmic fiction, it's a thoughtless system that just barely resists anthropomorphism. It's not like us. The Earth is a great, ancient thing that can destroy all we value for no reason other than our own greed. We dug up too many fossils, we climbed mountains for bragging rights, we read Shelley's *Ozymandias* and thought, *But I could build a better statue.* Just as the sand consumed all the works of that most ironic king of kings, it will harvest our material and transform us into something better suited for future life on Earth. Something humble and without the concept of ownership. Something animal or, even better, something dead.

FIVE LITRES

Robert Lepage's production of Béla Bartók's *Bluebeard's Castle* has me thinking about blood. That's not particularly strange, given the opera essentially consists of the titular beardo showing his new wife, Judith, seven chambers within his castle, all but one of which contain the sticky red stuff that's best kept in our veins. It's a plasmic opera on the page, and this particular version is especially visceral. When he opens the final door, a pool of blood opens under the proscenium, out of which climb Bluebeard's three previous brides, once dressed in white and now painted crimson with slick, salty, potentially infectious ichor.

I admit that I recoiled when I saw it. I'm not a person who generally finds the sight of blood off-putting. I don't faint at the sight of my own wounds, and for as long as I can remember, I've enjoyed blood's metallic tang, that iron flavour of a bit tongue or a lost baby tooth. I like my steak rare. But such abundance! To fill six castle chambers, to create a full pool of life fluid—it becomes too much semiotically. As the procession slithers across the stage, leaving claret snail trails behind the trains of their wedding dresses, I can't help but wonder that most terrible red-carpet cliché: who are you wearing?

An adult human, on average, contains five litres of blood. For reference, that's five small milk cartons, or two full Kool-Aid juice pitchers. How many people does it take to fill an elevator at the Overlook Hotel? To flood Beverly Marsh's bathroom? To cover Bluebeard's garden or to maintain his pool? Rivers of blood, oceans of blood, a hellish bloody rain that fills up gutters and coagulates on the edges of sewer drains. The possibility demands a new metric, one inclusive of individuality while also acknowledging groups. We need to appreciate blood as population. Five litres is a person, ten is a couple, fifteen is company, twenty's a crowd.

FIGHTING GHOSTS

My head is a haunted dojo.

When I close my eyes, my mind defies geography, geometry, and time. In my bed, at my desk, in a crowd of people in downtown Toronto, the memory can consume me, suck me in with force. My writhing post-traumatic anxiety, collected in a pulsing red orb deep in my core, expands outward to create a nightmare world, flexing and vibrating as I clench my teeth. Humidity. Heat. The roar of the ocean. I am on a pier in Costa Rica. My dad is there, but he's younger. And there's the man who shot him. Wide-eyed, panicked, angry, but knowing. I lived through this once.

The gun. I first thought it was a toy, baby blue with a brown handle—a .38 calibre snub nose. Now, it's a starter's pistol for an eternal bout. I was a black belt in karate, but the wide-eyed man shot my dad anyway.

Trapped in the memory, I fight my ghost nemesis. I do the special techniques Sensei taught me, the ones that break arms and trigger fingers, that rend revolvers from hands so you can throw them away or use them in self-defence. To shoot the attacker in his face and splatter his brains across the wooden decking holding us above the churning sea. Not for revenge, but with the hope that it might end these flashbacks.

In this spectral arena, even when I win the fight, reality course-corrects. *That's not what happened*. A sickening firework pop. The gun shoots a bullet into my father's chest and everything after fast-forwards—the screaming, the blood, the long walk carrying my fading dad. Then the diorama world squeezes in and resets. Humidity. Heat. Ocean roar. Wide eyes. Anger. Blue gun. Round two—fight!

You can't fight a ghost for the same reason you can't punch a tornado. They are climatological and you are corporeal. Martial arts is about the mastery of rules, while horror is about their exceptions. As a teenage karate instructor, when I saw Ghostface from *Scream* slicing through the youth of Woodsboro, my mind ran through the moves that would render the assailant useless. The way he projected his downward stabs? A high block, face strike, and takedown into an arm-break is all it would take to roll credits. But such thought experiments are done in bad faith, and the honest martial artist knows this. Immobilize Ghostface from *Scream* and find out the hard way that the killer is a persona consisting of multiple deranged sadists. Axe-kick the blob and learn how it feels to be digested alive, foot first. Fight the echo of the man who traumatized you and discover a million new shades of futility. Punch the tornado and know obliterating humility.

Perseverance. It was printed on the wall, above the mirrors that lined the front of the dojo. Sensei stood underneath it when he told the class about true martial arts mastery: the legendary tenth-degree black belt.

"It's only earned posthumously," he said. "Karate and self-defence—this is a lifelong journey. Black belt isn't the end, it's the beginning. You can learn all the moves in their right order, but there's always some way to improve your stance, your blocks, your side kicks."

"Kata" is the word for the traditional form of karate. A sequence of techniques that, when performed with proper intensity and proficiency, tells the story of a fight. To watch a black belt perform a kata is to see a person fend off a series of attackers and leave no survivors. To be a black belt performing a kata is to defend yourself from the echoes of ancient narrative tradition, visualizing a kick from a long-dead opponent and deflecting his leg with a perfect low block.

The objective of karate is enlightenment through fearlessness. To walk the Earth and know that whatever chaos you are confronted with, you can meet it with confidence. That's the point of fighting all those ghosts, over and over. Always blocking first, then punching, kicking, throwing, and screaming a *kiai* for extra-explosive power. Always bowing when it's done, ready to repeat the fight, understanding each kata as part of a larger sequence, a string of events iterating in defiance of chaos: one giant brawl you take on against ghosts—until you become one.

100 SECONDS TO MIDNIGHT

"When someone asks if you're a god, you say: yes!"
—Winston Zeddemore, *Ghostbusters* (1984)

Last I heard, the Doomsday Clock is one hundred seconds to midnight. Nuclear war looms while the climate crisis sets the globe ablaze. According to the Bulletin of the Atomic Scientists who move the clock's hands, ongoing information warfare and the erosion of international political infrastructure have hampered society's ability to further delay the apocalypse. They describe the emergency as "an absolutely unacceptable state of world affairs that has eliminated any margin for error or further delay." The seals are open and the horsemen are saddling up. It's about to get biblical and there's nothing we can do about it. Yet it's somehow still inappropriate for me to scream at work.

That's why I'm jealous of the Ghostbusters. They also toil under the shadow of the apocalypse, but at least they get to holler about it. Chased out of the New York Public Library by a free-floating, full-torso, vaporous apparition; getting slimed by a focused non-terminal repeating phantasm in the Sedgewick Hotel—they're constantly in over their heads and expressing their fear in wailing harmony. Ray Stantz, Peter Venkman, Egon Spengler, and Winston Zeddemore are small business workers grinding away with a clear view of the end times, paying bills and clocking in, without anything close to a long-term plan for actually preventing Judgment Day. They're role models for the short-term contract economy.

Heroes for those of us trapped in capitalism as it devours our world via flame, radiation, and superhurricanes.

The Ghostbusters are on the clock almost the entire movie, even as armageddon starts to burrow out of the Big Apple—bustin' ain't free. They're still working during the climactic confrontation on a Manhattan high-rise where a portal has opened to a hostile dimension, bringing forth the destruction god Gozer. In his work uniform, staring into the red eyes of annihilation, Ray attempts to parlay with the deity on behalf of his client, the City of New York.

"Are you a god?" asks Gozer.

"No," says Ray. And the team is set to screaming again. Violently electrocuted by spectral lightning bolts shot from Gozer's outstretched fingertips, Ray and his colleagues writhe in pain, and while it sounds violent on paper, it's actually funny and relatable. Sure, it didn't work out, but at least he tried.

That Stantzian futility is part of a long tradition. William Hope Hodgson's Carnacki the Ghost Finder, H. P. Lovecraft's Randolph Carter, Shirley Jackson's Dr. John Montague—there's a centuries-long cultural lineage of curious minds making a living by simply encountering unexplainable phenomena and screaming, fainting, or, at best, fencing it off from innocent lives. John Constantine, Mulder and Scully, the Winchesters, Winona Earp—even the coolest modern iterations of the occult detective end up getting by on half-measures. The living can't kill what's already dead. Sending a demon back to Hell is just short-term supernatural house arrest. Closing a portal to an evil dimension is the equivalent of boarding up a window against an eternally raging storm. Call it fate, call it karma, call it professional procrastination. When the brimstone starts falling, even the most intrepid intellectuals can't gig their way to safety.

The Ghostbusters carry on this tradition of existential toil. Sure, "ghostbusting" sounds violent and final, and the trappings of the No Ghosts brand borrow from the pest-control aesthetic, but Ghostbusters and their franchisees can't do much more than find a ghost, trap it, and move its essence to a containment unit. They face the maddening state of the world near its end, understand they have limited influence over it, and compartmentalize. They can't win, but that doesn't dampen their hustle.

You don't need to solve a problem to make things better. Sometimes, you just need to get in harm's way to help out. Contain the trouble, absorb the shocks, reason with the transdimensional entity—take one for the team. So, if you one day find yourself facing down an ancient Sumarian deity on a skyscraper with a positron collider strapped to your back, flanked by your ghostbusting co-workers, remember that human insignificance is the stuff of champions. Don't be afraid to scream at work. It's okay if you're not a god—just fake it till you make it.

METAPHYSICAL GRAFFITI

Stigmata

Arthur peeled a wet red Band-Aid off the tip of his ring finger, revealing the mark. Blood oozed from a deep cut in his callus, a bright cherry bursting in the early May sun, all the more brilliant in contrast with our white Catholic high school uniforms.

"It kills," he said. "I can't even play anymore and it's driving me nuts."

I marvelled at the wound. The night before, Arthur told me he'd played "Stairway to Heaven" along with the CD. Perfectly. And the song left its imprint. I figured it was the set of bended triplets near the end of the solo that did it, the sheer amount of friction during the most impossible part of Jimmy Page's magnum opus. I imagined Arthur's Elixir string, with its special nanoweb coating, slicing through his fingertip like a cheese cutter as he pushed the metal thread against the fretboard to make his instrument wail. I pictured streaks of sticky blood smearing the neck of his Gibson electric guitar, his refusal to stop powered by the singularity of his accomplishment. The revelry of finally playing the perfect song. I was jealous.

That night, I sat in my parents' basement alone, between stacks of amplifiers. Classic rock records adorned the walls, including Led Zeppelin's fourth studio album, the unspeakable one named with sacred geometry instead of letters. Pouring over photocopied music sheets in my red three-ring binder, my black Washburn in my lap, I tried to warp my fingers in the right ways to summon the song through the mesh of my amplifier. I wanted to conjure it through ritual, perfectly, like Arthur had, so I could be marked too.

Hail, Paimon!

Human ego death is the core of occult horror. Our rational, explainable, known world abuts the abyssal land beyond our map's edge, and the occult is what creeps over the border from the dark side. Cultists are turncoats against humanity: hijacked by malevolent ideology, given over to the demonic, occupying corporeal space on behalf of a half-glimpsed metaphysical revelation.

Ari Aster's 2018 film *Hereditary* is a case study in the species betrayal of cultists. The movie is a brutal depiction of grief, in which the Graham family confronts the death of Leigh, their matriarch, and the seemingly accidental decapitation of her favourite grandchild, Charlie. The surviving family—Annie; her husband, Steve; and their other child, Peter—experience bone-chilling phenomena as they mourn. Ghosts appear, members of the family sleepwalk, and Leigh's grave is desecrated. Eventually, Steve is burned alive in a plume of magical flame, Annie beheads herself with a piano wire, and Peter becomes the host body for Paimon, one of the eight sub-princes of Hell.

On a first viewing, it seems like the Grahams are being tortured by a single entity, Paimon, who is represented by a shining light. But most of what happens in the film is the work of Paimon's human fan club. Even in *Hereditary*'s masterful final sequence—when Peter finds the crispy corpse of his father in the middle of the night as he walks through the house, failing to notice all the grinning naked humans hiding in the shadows who are waiting to pounce— it's nearly impossible to comprehend the cultists as human. And for all intents and purposes, they are nothing more than fleshy, nude extensions of Paimon himself, desperate drones and workers to his terrible queen bee.

A second viewing lays bare the cult's machinations—the symbols they carve to summon Paimon's influence in specific places, the social manipulation they deploy to get Annie to read a magic spell that will help materialize their dark master. But even when their movements and vandalism can be delineated, the cultists in *Hereditary* work in such full dedication to an anti-human force that they feel like an evil metaphysical presence. The goal of supplicancy, after all, is self-negation in favour of the worshipped divine, to abandon your agency and don the performance of possession. It's liberation from the responsibility of existing: you cannot be credited for your service to an overlord from beyond the pale. Dancing to a demonic tune, changing the world on behalf of the non-corporeal through meticulous ritual—if anyone asks, the devil made you do it.

Here's to My Sweet Satan

There's a hidden message in "Stairway to Heaven." If you play the verse about the "spring clean for the May Queen" backwards, Robert Plant inhales Satanic reverse lyrics:

> *Here's to my sweet Satan*
> *The one whose little path would make me sad*
> *Whose power is Satan*
> *He will give those with him 666*
> *There was a little toolshed where he made us suffer*
> *Sad Satan*

And that's why, whenever I hear the delicate picking of the introduction, or the rousing pagan lyrics of the second movement, the intoxicating descent of the solo, or the climactic breakdown with its references to alchemy and hidden messages, I think about my favourite classic rock band being tortured near the shores of Loch Ness, on an estate once owned by Aleister Crowley.

Crowley once said Boleskine House seemed purpose-built for the demon-summoning ritual described in a grimoire titled *The Sacred Magic of Abramelin the Mage*. The text details a six-month operation intended to call forth evil spirits and bind them to a magician's will. Satan, Lucifer, Belial, Leviathan, and their sub-princes, Astarot, Magot, Asmodee, Beelzebub, Oriens, Ariton, Amaimon, and Paimon, are conjured into the property's tool shed and commanded from a safe distance. Crowley attempted the Abramelin spell at least once, but was interrupted halfway through when called away to attend urgent secret society matters in London before the demonic six-moon period could birth evil princes into his makeshift backyard incubator. After that, local rumours suggested that devils roamed the surrounding moors, casting hexes and bringing death. Conspiracy theorists even posit the Loch Ness Monster is the result of Crowley's abandoned Abramelin procedure.

Jimmy Page purchased Boleskine in 1970 and owned it during the composition and recording of "Stairway to Heaven." That's what gives the backwards message its horrible context. Sure, the hidden lyrics certainly don't sound recorded on purpose, and they do read a bit like nonsense, but it's the same kind of "nonsense" contained in one centuries-old grimoire that claims to bridge the gap between our world and that of King Paimon and Sweet Satan. The band denies the message in the May Queen verse exists, despite Robert Plant's earlier lyric about words having two meanings, but that doesn't diminish the uncanny connections that make the song sound so magical.

The surviving members of Led Zeppelin don't talk about the occult at all, let alone entertain theories about the backwards sounds on "Stairway." And that's why the dark myths about the band's Boleskine connection have survived decades of rock journalism, Satanic panic, and the secret-killing power of the Internet. Ironically, these same forces defanged Zeppelin's scary contemporaries, who actively exploited horror imagery. Black Sabbath was name-dropped by the Son of Sam and beloved by real Satan worshippers, but now guitarist Tony Iommi ponders the occult with a weary curiosity in interviews. Alice Cooper got his stage name from a Ouija board and was banned from playing in Australia, thanks to his horror-flavoured theatrical hijinks, but today he's a born-again Christian with a syndicated radio show. We know so much about scary bands that they seem disappointing. But Zeppelin was different. They always tried to keep their machinations from public view, even now only reluctantly talking about their most legendary days in the 1970s—and their mythology thrives.

Obsession and the occult feed off each other, empowered by gaps in information. The fanatic fills in those gaps, connecting push-pins and photographs and maps and news clippings with stretchy red yarn. After a while, the adjacent nature of arcane knowledge and the rapture of obscure association can feel like true revelation. Linking the threads of Jimmy Page's ownership of Boleskine to the composition of "Stairway to Heaven," to references to Satan and shedlike structures mentioned in both the backwards message and Abramelin's text, to parallel misfortunes between Crowley's confidants and Robert Plant's loved ones, to overt references to the haunted "Stairway" verse on Plant's 2017 solo album, despite his insistence that he hates the song—it's not just the abundance of data points, it's the length of the yarn connecting them.

That's why I think of my record collection when I watch *Hereditary*, a film about the Abramelin ritual gone wrong. Caught in a web of conspiracy connections, I can't help but imagine the suffering of Led Zeppelin in 1970, according to the tortured backward gasps of their singer, who claims his record player spins in only one direction.

The Great God Pan

"I only like songs with screaming in them."

Nick was in control of the stereo, sitting shotgun in our mom's purple Acura on a two-hour car ride through Southern Ontario farmland. Mom piloted us past orderly cornfields carved out of murky forest, the landscape punctuated by marshmallowy bales of hay wrapped in white plastic and barns in various states of disrepair. In the back seat, I was at the mercy of *Nix Mix*, a burned CD filled with Napstered tracks by Linkin Park and Godsmack.

"I promise there's screaming in this," I said, pushing the jewel case of *Led Zeppelin IV* across the console separating the front seats. "Just listen to one song. Track four."

Begrudgingly, he ejected his bootlegged nu metal compilation and fed the new disc into the dashboard. Jimmy Page's delicate plucking wove together with the layered recorder melody played by John Paul Jones.

"Just wait," I said. The song filled the car for eight minutes. When it was over, Nick played it again. And again. The remainder of the trip, we listened to "Stairway to Heaven" without comment as Mom drove. That was the day he began to change.

As I hermitted away in our basement back home, poring over musical notes like spells and polluting the air with misshapen copies of the song I knew so perfectly in my mind, Nick's hair grew longer. He started wearing T-shirts with the fallen angel Lucifer on them, printed under the name of the band we now both idolized. I unplugged my guitar, silently moving in ritual practice, vowing only to electrify my instrument when my imitation was as flawless as the song piping through my brother's omnipresent headphones. We faded into clouds of sonic and visual vandalism, each of us a simulacrum of an ideal revealed to us through "Stairway to Heaven."

"It's Cousin Itt," Dad said at the dinner table when Nick's hair had reached his shoulders, hiding his face. But the moniker didn't stick. My brother's golden locks were too wild and untameable. They demanded pagan celebration. As our extended family came to accept the new Nick, the natural comparison emerged. He looked just like Robert Plant. Meanwhile, my fingers ached, the spell struggling to manifest through me.

My brother and I presented as fans, but really we were disappearing, given over to a tune, saturated in song, called by the piper. We listened hard, just as the lyrics instruct, hoping an arcane truth would emerge from the gaps between the notes. We hoped the spirits of our worshipped idols would possess us, so that one day I could pluck my guitar's strings and make people hear Jimmy Page, or part the curtains of Nick's hair to reveal someone else entirely. Cultists, we abandoned our egos to become vessels for our new gods.

SILENT RUINS

P.T. is legendary. Launched for free on PlayStation 4 in August 2014 under a shroud of mystery, the acronym stands for "Playable Teaser," though what it was marketing was anyone's guess, given that the developers published it under a pseudonym. The entire "game," if that's what you want to call it, takes place in a small section of a suburban home touched with the signs of prolonged domestic abuse. You're trapped in the haunted first floor of a house that is lit by sconces, decorated with pictures of a smiling family, carpeted by empty liquor bottles and half-empty pill blister-packs. And you're not alone. A ghost named Lisa, a towering, spasming, moaning apparition, stalks you in your quest to find an exit. Occasionally, Lisa pounces, brutalizes you, dismembers you. But even in death there is no escape. When she's all done carving you up, you reawaken in the same corridors, set back to searching.

The space is simple enough: an initial stretch from your starting point to a window, then a right turn into a two-storey foyer with a door to a destitute bathroom, beyond which you can see a desk with a radio on it and the house's locked entrance. A small lantern hangs from the ceiling by a chain. The whole thing terminates in a short flight of stairs descending to a basement door, and when you walk through it, you end up right where you started. By walking in an L shape and going down some stairs, you end up traversing a flat circle. It's unsettling as hell.

But *P.T.*'s uncanny geography is only its second-most disturbing architectural feature. The real fright-maker is the game's one corner that necessitates the right turn into the foyer. Every iteration of the hallway has the potential for some small change to manifest beyond the corner. Sometimes the bathroom door is open, sometimes the radio is playing a report about a string of familicides committed by fathers, sometimes the lights are out. The lantern in the foyer is red and swinging violently, or it's replaced by a hanging refrigerator that's dripping blood as a child screams inside. Sometimes, Lisa is standing there, gurgling, and moaning, and staring.

The corner is a pure, distilled horror machine. The intimacy of the domestic space and the repetition of the right-turn motion as you cycle through the hallway builds expectation. Turning the corner reinforces familiarity, only to break it with an unexpected variation on your next pass through. You walk and turn and walk and turn and walk and turn and eventually you learn the horrible truth: when you can't predict what comes next based on past experience, it's all new. What seemed cyclical was linear the whole time. I thought I was walking in a strange, misshapen circle, but it was actually a downward spiral, a terrible, descending infinity.

Sometimes the thought of infinity can make you feel insignificant, but that's because you're not thinking big enough. When *P.T.* launched, everyone played it simultaneously, all over the world, creating a multiverse of never-ending haunted halls inside video game consoles. Identical character models walked through identical homes to be met with identical horrors. And while that simultaneity is true of any popular video game, *P.T.* depended on that cosmic parallel for its mystery to be solved. The pseudonymous developers left out puzzle pieces, so any one player couldn't find the solution. Clues scattered throughout the game were written in different languages, forcing collaboration outside of the game space.

Players took to Reddit and YouTube and Twitch in a large-scale meta-collaboration, translating and deciphering clues, building a bigger picture of what *P.T.* was, until a solution was finally stumbled upon: a meticulous midnight ritual that involves taking a precise number of steps, pausing for specific amounts of time, and speaking into a microphone hooked up to your controller. Doing this just right causes a phone to ring, and when you pick it up, the basement door opens and the teaser reveals its true nature: *P.T.* was the first taste of *Silent Hills*, a new entry in the infamous multimedia horror franchise co-directed by Hideo Kojima and Guillermo del Toro, starring Norman Reedus from *The Walking Dead*.

Suddenly, all of *P.T.*'s horrific ambiguity clicked into a history and mythology. The association with *Silent Hills* gave the spiral halls weight and an association with punishment. Previous nightmares—poor souls torn apart by psychosexual manifestations of their crimes, ancient evils summoned to taint the banality of small-town America—recontextualized the horrors beyond that one corner. I was just one of infinite Normans walking the halls, partaking in a grand tradition of penance through suffering. By accepting that none of our experiences was wholly unique, we unlocked a greater truth: we were all trapped in one of many private hells, and all over the world we celebrated together as we sat alone.

About three-quarters of the way to the ritual that makes the phone ring and ends the game, the player experiences a scripted crash. The screen starts to glitch, a slowed-down voice begins reading numbers, and you are presented with one of eight error messages with tongue-in-cheek references to "inexplicable bugs" and games being unable to hurt you in real life. The game goes through a fake restart before bringing you to the final hallway configuration.

Despite the impressively spooky narrative design, incompleteness is the defining quality of *P.T.* Less than a year after the teaser's release, Konami—the major game studio attached to the project—cancelled *Silent Hills*, severed ties with Kojima, and scrubbed every trace of the game from the online marketplace. Now the only way to experience *P.T.* is on PS4 systems that had it installed before May 2015. And if you walk the now-rarified halls long enough, you will find small details that imply something bigger, a larger purpose.

In 2019, researcher Lance McDonald found a way to modify his copy of *P.T.* and exit the hallway, to stroll through a small section of Silent Hill that Kojima and del Toro's team constructed outside the bounds of the initial play experience. Watching McDonald's brief tour of an unfinished game is an exercise in frustration. As he examines disused apartment buildings and abandoned vehicles, one gets a sense of a grand design, something that, if we could put our heads together like we had in the hallway to bridge impossible gaps and solve impossible puzzles, we might unlock some greater meaning to all our strange nightmares. But that aura of purpose is nothing more than a foggy miasma clinging to the ruins of *Silent Hills*. Left to make meaning from abandonment, all that remains is the ghost, the corner, the ambience, the meaningless punishment—those infinite Norman Reeduses in an eternal, twisting descent.

WHERE THE CREEPYPASTAS ARE

Jeff the Killer has no nose, and he cut off his eyelids too. His red mouth looks like it's sliced into his face, and you can summon him into your home at night when you're alone in your bedroom. Just chant his name—"Jeff the Killer, Jeff the Killer, Jeff the Killer"—until he appears and proceeds to slaughter your family, uttering his famous catchphrase, "Shhh... Go to sleep."

I got this information by googling it. Jeff's details are copied and pasted across a series of fandom wikis along with a smattering of other J the K trivia. Thirteen years old, his favourite food is sushi, and his hobbies include murder, stalking and "messing around." According to my suggested search queries, other people commonly look up Jeff's zodiac sign. Google says he's a Gemini, but I think that's a category error. The search engine must be conflating noseless Jeff with famous May baby Jeffrey Dahmer. What's undeniable, though, is that Jeff the Killer murdered his parents, snuffed out his bullies, and is a confirmed, real-deal Creepypasta.

Creepypasta wasn't always a type of monster. The term is still widely used to describe a memetic form of folk-lore—stories or images—that grew from the Internet. It's a spooky derivation of "copypasta," a webspeak perversion of "copy-paste," referring to the practice of duplicating text and proliferating it without attribution across forums, chat rooms, email chains, and blogs. The effect was a new horror mythology containing video game cartridges haunted by drowned boys, mysterious staircases encountered in forests that drive people insane, the infamous Slenderman, and our bloodthirsty friend Jeff. At some point along the way, creepypasta became synonymous with a certain type of monster: pale, violent ghouls with unspecific modes of operation and canonical favourite foods. Ergo, Jeff is a creepypasta monster born from creepypasta lore.

It's messy and nearly impossible to map. The information is iterated across countless text fields, scattered throughout cyberspace, contradicted, disputed, and remixed. It's goofy and overburdened with explanations and controversial characters that some net-lorists believe undercut the purity of creepypasta despite clearly being loved and supported by legions of wiki users. It's juvenile, mostly, but that's okay because creepypasta is curated by children.

No one uses the Internet like twelve-year-olds, and that's never more apparent than in Irene Taylor Brodsky's documentary *Beware the Slenderman*, which investigates the 2014 stabbing of Payton Leutner by her fellow preteens Anissa Weier and Morgan Geyser. The assailants lured Leutner into the woods under the pretense of playing hide-and-seek, perforated the girl with nineteen knife wounds, and fled the scene. A cop found Weier and Geyser and brought them to the station, where two detectives questioned the girls separately about the attempted murder. The ensuing conversations are unbelievable.

Weier and Geyser confess to their crime and motive: they had to sacrifice Leutner in order to gain the affection of Slenderman, king of the creepypastas, and gain access to the Slender Mansion where the rest of the uncanny noodles live. The police, clearly unfamiliar with pretty much every proper noun coming out of their suspects' mouths, start drowning in Internet esoterica. Interrogating two real girls in two separate rooms, attempting to learn why twelve-year-olds would try to brutally kill their friend, the investigators are fed a semi-fictional narrative based on poorly written Internet ghost stories. So they have to treat creepypasta as real.

Every time I watch those scenes, I put myself in the position of the police, hearing terms like Slender Mansion and creepypasta for the first time, while trying to solve a brutal assault. What do they imagine when they hear these girls say, with full conviction, that they were going to meet someone or something named Slenderman? Do the adults, even for a second, think any part of the mythology unfurling before them is real? It's a pure Lovecraftian dark age for the cops.

Then I put myself in the position of Geyser and Weier, which is a lot easier. Once, I was a lonely twelve-year-old on the Internet too. I looked up images of corpses, I anonymously logged on to chat rooms and pretended to be older. I went on magic websites and printed off instructions for summoning familiars or controlling the elements. And it wasn't so much that I thought those things were real out of naïveté; I wanted to believe in them out of fantastical desperation. I wanted the world I saw online to be real, and between my developing brain and the screen of my parents' Compaq Presario, there was nothing to stop me. No contradictory information. No skeptical debunking. No parents to contextualize it. Just like those girls, I scoured the Internet for monsters, found what I was looking for, and let it shape my reality.

Come to think of it, maybe everyone uses the Internet like twelve-year-olds.

Walls don't matter anymore. Not the way they used to. We built them to keep the wild things out—wolves and bears, mosquitoes and ticks, stormy weather. The home used to be sacred ground. Vampires couldn't enter without an invitation. But now, as Emma and I stroll around our Halifax block in the wake of Hurricane Dorian, a Category 2 storm that toppled trees, ripped off roofs, and collapsed a crane downtown, I notice digital blue light splashing on window-panes. It flickers from square portals opened on purpose by residents as they let another kind of outside in—a dimension composed of tickering social media feeds and streaming video and reportage.

The narrow street, lined with colourful wood-panel houses, seems to exist on an island of darkness. Most of the city's power is still out and the end of the road looks like interstellar space. We pass a slim calico meowing at her owner's door, pawing the frame.

"I'm relieved I grew up when I did," I say, "before the Internet turned into a radicalization machine."

Emma shakes her head. We've discussed this anxiety before. Older millennials talk about the accelerated evolution of communication technology as an ongoing trauma. Our brains are dense archives of all the different ways we sat alone throughout our adolescence, and the myriad graphical interfaces we stared at to socialize—ICQ, MSN, AOL if you had a friend in the States. Chat rooms on video game servers, role-playing forums where adults and children collectively pretended to be *Star Wars* characters, close calls with abduction, virtual puberty fuelled by jpeg porn and crude attempts at cybersex with strangers. Magic spells and bomb-making instructions. Pictures of dead bodies. Flash animations on eBaum's World about all the hidden messages in Disney movies. None of it contextualized by adults because it was new to them too, if they encountered it at all. We talk about the Internet now to turn our solitary memories of growing up in cyber-wilderness into something shareable, to validate unwitnessed time, like an existential support group for half of a generation. And sometimes that means airing fears.

"I know you're worried you'd be a lobster," says Emma. "But it doesn't work that way."

She's right. On this point, she always is. Emma knows the lobsters—anonymous pods of Internet-dwelling conservatives obsessed with order, chauvinistic hierarchy, and clean bedrooms—aren't just confused youth, they're adults too, looking for a guide to corroborate the negative feelings that grow in the light of connected screens. But I still worry, sometimes, that if I had to live my life again I'd grow up into a human crustacean, some poor impressionable soul ensnared by prescriptivist manifesto mongers with YouTube channels and self-help books who pedal cures for chaos, summoned into bedrooms like Jeff the Killer, infecting brains with anger, hate, and selfishness. Irrational, sure, but when recollecting long-past trauma, one looks at all the sheer cliff edges they narrowly avoided by the grace of luck and wonders, what if...

My fear of being lobsterfied in a hypothetical alternate youth is an expression of gratitude. It could have been so much worse. I survived adolescence on a desert island of information technology with my empathy intact. In a dark-mirror universe, I picture a hardened, beastly me—Pinchy Pete—beclawed and distrusting of others, made that way from typing into online voids and connecting with monsters instead of friends.

Reaching the end of the street, Emma and I turn our backs on the darkness. Walking home the way we came, hand in hand, we pass the calico curled up on her owner's doorstep. Don't worry, little cat, it's better out here. There's a new wilderness inside those walls, filled with killer teens and Slendermen. It's a wild rumpus in there, behind locked doors. We're better out here with the storms.

BROKEN NIGHTMARE TELEPHONE

Mostly, I remember the pressure on my neck and the weight of an adult man pressing down on me. I sat in the green upholstered office chair at the family computer desk as Dad hugged me from behind. It was more like a headlock, but the message was clear.

"Granddad died," he said.

The white, grey, and teal light from the computer screen blurred through my gathering tears. Dad didn't cry, but he wasn't really breathing either. We knew Granddad was on his way out; he'd suffered multiple heart attacks during back surgery and was forced to endure an extended tenure in the intensive care unit. Last I'd heard, the old man still thought World War II was on. I figured he must have confused London, Ontario, for its British counterpart, as he spent time near there as a lieutenant in the Canadian navy. During one hospital visit, he screamed at my dad to set him free.

After the funeral, my brain went haywire. Undiagnosed bipolar II disorder turned my grief into a maelstrom of depression and low-key mania. I started missing school because I couldn't get out of bed, and when I did go to class I sometimes saw shadows in my peripheral vision, people standing in places I knew were empty. During a depressive low point one afternoon, I ripped my belt from the loops on my jeans, wrapped it around my neck, and tried to hang myself from the wooden post at the foot of my bed. Darkness gathered in my vision, my blood pounded like a timpani in my temples, and guilt saved my life. How selfish, I thought, to inflict more loss on my family just so I could feel better. The memory of Granddad stood monolithic in my mind, towering over my teenage suicide attempt.

In the aftermath, I learned my mood disorder was hereditary. Dad had it too. Who knows if his parents did, since the Greatest Generation wasn't exactly open about emotional vulnerability. I went to a psychiatrist and a therapist, and life resumed under the promise I would never try to kill myself again. But the miasma of my attempted suicide lingered in my bedroom, the memory of a darkest moment narrowly averted, and the heavy shame that came with it. At night, sometimes I had trouble sleeping, and I fixated on the shadows in the corner near my closet.

One night, the darkness in that corner stretched a little farther, drew my gaze deeper into the blackness. I strained my eyes to focus. Fear gripped my diaphragm, halted my breath, turned me into a statue. The excess shadow was the figure of a man, tall and grim. He stood for a moment, watching me, before crossing the room in three quick steps, throwing his hands around my throat, and strangling me. He screamed in my face, and I tried to scream back. Mostly, I remember the pressure on my neck and the weight of an adult man pressing down on me.

I told my brother about the encounter in my bedroom, and he shared his own ghost stories. Once, he said, he woke up on the couch in the basement to see the spectre of a little girl tracing her finger on the coffee table. Another time, I roused the whole family by sleepwalking to the upright piano kept in the hallway outside the upstairs bedrooms and playing its keys in the dark, my pale form visible from Nick's open door as I tapped away on middle C. Talking can be a form of exorcism, and my conversation with Nick worked as a protection ritual. My encounter with the shadow strangler remained a singular event.

Years passed, and Nick and I both moved away from home, becoming roommates in Toronto. I worked at a chocolate store in the mall; he worked at the harbour downtown. We both went to school in the fall, unhaunted. Until, returning from a visit to our parents' house one weekend, Nick sat me down on our couch.

"Something extremely messed up happened when I was at home," he said. "I was staying in your old room and—I swear to God this is true—I couldn't get to sleep and I kept staring at this shadow in the corner. Then it morphed into an old man, and he came at me and grabbed me and started screaming in my face. It was insane. I swear, I wasn't sleeping. I wasn't even drunk or high. I can't explain it."

"Nick," I said. "Don't you remember? After Granddad died, that same thing happened to me."

We had no hypothesis beyond the paranormal, which we dismissed outright, given we were both caught up in the new atheist trend that was gaining popularity. Sycophantic in our admiration for the likes of Richard Dawkins, Christopher Hitchens, and Neil deGrasse Tyson, we agreed there must be a scientific explanation for the phenomenon. But we didn't have enough data to draw a feasible, secular conclusion (also, we were fine arts students).

The information we needed for a working theory didn't stay hidden for long. Next time I slept in my old bedroom, I saw the angry man in the shadows; he throttled me on the mattress and he screamed in my face. I told Nick, and when he visited home a few weeks later, he slept in my room and reported his experience back to me. Back and forth, we took turns like this, each telling the other of our last encounter. Any new detail we noticed in a confrontation became part of the mythology of our shared ghost, and eventually we began to understand what was happening: we were hosts to a violent memetic phantom passing between us. Each time we told the story, we enabled the reproduction and variation that provides the basis for evolution. Our game of broken nightmare telephone sustained the dark avatar of grief, guilt, and anger.

Learning the name of my near-fatal mood disorder allowed me to understand it and to see when it was affecting my thoughts and behaviour. In the same way, using the language of memology helped Nick and me to compartmentalize and describe our strangle-ghost encounters. We knew what was happening when the monster was in the room, and even began to anticipate each frightful episode. Still, just as knowing I have bipolar II doesn't make it go away, the ability to describe our shadow tormentor did nothing to curb his violence.

We lived with our shared ghost and continued to talk about it, even though we knew our discussions doomed the other to a sleepless night in our parents' guest room. As time went on, and we moved into different homes, the haunting became a sweet, albeit morbid, family history. We accepted the origin of the strangle-man as manifesting from the guilt and grief around Granddad's death and my subsequent turmoil. This was how we engaged in the difficult parts of our familial narrative, through conversation in a language at the intersection of spiritualism and pop-science.

One spring morning, everything changed. We were both at the breakfast table in our parents' house, and Nick, who'd slept in the guest room the night before, wobbled between excitement and exhaustion. His hair was a blond thornbush. Bags hung under his bright eyes as we sipped black coffee.

"It happened. Only this time it was different."

He couldn't sleep, he said. And that's when he felt the telltale dread. Recognizing the advent of the shadowy man, he covered his head with blankets to block the coming on-slaught of sensory hallucinations. And it worked. He got to sleep, hidden under the bedspread, until he next woke. Uncovering his head, he beheld a man's silhouette between him and the room's one moonlit window. He shut his eyes, and a voice spoke his name. Still, he managed to fall back to sleep. His familiarity, he said, must have given him a critical distance from the events.

But Nick woke a third time, and though the shadow was gone and no voice whispered his name, he was fully uncov-ered, his right arm pressed to the wall above the headboard by some invisible force. He couldn't move. He couldn't scream. Pinned to the wall, he suffered in silence.

"Well," I said. "That's a lot more difficult to explain."

Working through the new data, we conscripted our mom, a speech and language pathologist with experience in psychology. We explained the history of our memetic haunting, its emotional roots, and how the nightmare evolved over time. We told her about the pressure around our necks and the weight of a man pressing down on us. She dismissed it outright.

"No, no," she said, leaning on the kitchen counter with her elbows. "It's probably just your father sleepwalking."

FEAR OF THE SHARK

"All this machine does is swim and eat and make little sharks. That's all."
—Matt Hooper, *Jaws* (1975)

There's no better monster than the shark. It's ancient and mysterious and made of teeth. A shark's skeleton is cartilaginous, decomposing after death so the only remains are jagged incisors. Its skin is covered in denticles, little aerodynamic stalagmites made of the same calcified tissue and enamel as its chompers. If you pet a shark with your bare hand in the wrong direction, it will shred your skin. That's why hardware manufacturers base their highest grades of sandpaper on shark skin—it's good for destroying.

Industrial designers aren't the only ones inspired by sharks. They've also sparked the imaginations of horror filmmakers looking to bridge the gap between fiction and reality. Sharks are nature's ready-made plug-and-play nightmare. The fewer modifications made, the better. The 1999 film *Deep Blue Sea* attempts to improve on the waterborne behemoths by giving them larger brains to, as per the movie poster, make them bigger, smarter, faster, and meaner. But the end result was goofy rather than scary. Sharks don't need to be improved upon with Hollywood mad science. Tinkering ruins perfection. Frame what nature gave us and let the creature do the rest.

Learn a bit more about sharks, and you find a majestic and social apex predator that actually wants nothing to do with the smorgasbord of human flesh bobbing in the water when we swim. Sharks don't eat people. Most encounters with the uberfish that result in human injury or death fall into the category experts call "bite and spit," in which a confused shark doesn't know what your naked arm or leg or midsection is, takes a sample, and then leaves you to bleed as it searches for something better.

Quint, the Ahabesque shark hunter in *Jaws*, has a show-stopping monologue near the film's halfway point. He describes the incident of the *USS Indianapolis*, the most infamous feeding frenzy of sharks on record. It's based on real events and precisely illustrates what makes sharks the ultimate crossover monster. Without embellishment, Quint shares memories of the sharks picking away at his fellow navy men, eating them alive with "doll's eyes" and a calm demeanour, emphasizing the fish's menace through understatement. He paints the picture of a monster through subtraction, not addition.

The sharks described in Quint's monologue in *Jaws* did eat people, since food is scarce for animals in the open ocean. But the real killer (discounting the Japanese submariners who slammed two torpedoes into the *Indianapolis*) is the ocean. Sailors died of thirst, hunger, exposure, and salt toxicity. The sharks were there, but it's hard to find consistent data indicating they contributed significantly to the death toll.

The cold bodies of water that cover our planet are deadly. In terms of all the unintentional ways to die on this planet, drowning in oceans, lakes, and rivers is the third most common. Approximately 372,000 people drown every year, according to the World Health Organization. You're more likely to accidentally drown in natural water than to choke to death on food, burn to death in a fire, or die from exposure to sharp objects—and that statistic excludes shark teeth. The fact is, in the past fifty years, fewer than three thousand people total were attacked by unprovoked sharks, and the vast majority didn't even die. Compared to its saline environment, the shark is a tame scapegoat. It's a convenient container through which to funnel our fears. It's a set of oceanic jaws when we need a beast to blame. Even though we should be scared of the water instead.

AUDIENT VOID, AUTHORIAL VOID

The camera destroys us.

—

Found-footage horror is fragmentary by nature. It imposes narrative limits—the footage being watched is important to a larger story but is incomplete. The characters onscreen and the camera operators aren't trying to make the movie you're watching. To Heather, Mike, and Josh, *The Blair Witch Project* was supposed to be a creepy documentary, not an artifact of their annihilation.

—

Heather &
Mike &
Josh &
[Footage not found]

—

It's pretty standard that studios don't even try to pretend found-footage movies are real anymore. And that's understandable, considering it's a huge ask for an audience to imagine the film they are seeing about real people getting killed by supernatural forces is a) playing in a theatre or on a paid streaming service, and b) only rated 14A. All horror films require some suspension of disbelief, but ironically, found footage—which aspires to do the work of suspending your disbelief for you—requires the biggest initial ask: please forget this movie you're watching is a movie at all.

Forget it was engineered by filmmakers who screened it at festivals. Forget it was purchased and distributed by multi-million-dollar production companies. Forget this entertainment is entertainment.

That's not true of *Petscop*, a YouTube series about a haunted PlayStation game, presented in the popular Let's Play format. Across a series of twenty-five videos, we see gameplay of the titular *Pokemon* knock-off played by Paul, the narrator, as he slowly connects the macabre details of the unfinished game's hidden areas—torture devices, graves marking dead children, oracular text fields—to his own life. It's dense, fragmentary, and gloriously anonymous. The self-publishing nature of YouTube allows its contributors to recede from their art, in effect presenting *Petscop* unapologetically as a real artifact. There are no credits at the end of the footage or in the video description. No advertisements, no branded Twitter account. The video was introduced to the world through an in-character Reddit post from the same Paul popular for narrating his digital descent into retro gaming horror.

Petscop proves found footage is more than a camera style and a pretext. True found footage is self-annihilation as praxis, bestowing life unto art through one's own ego-death. If you want to make fiction that could be real, you need to exist like God: become unprovable.

—

Even when *Paranormal Activity* filmmaker Oren Peli managed to have his film distributed without ending credits, his name still had to appear on a two-paragraph title card, displayed after the final shot, stating he held the copyright and that the events of the photoplay were entirely fictitious.

The only reason I think *Petscop* isn't real is because I was told it's fake.

—

In a way, nothing we see on a screen is real. It's hard to admit, because so much of our world is experienced through shared video, photography, and field notes posted to social media feeds. But it's true, and not just in that David Foster Wallace TV-is-a-bunch-of-coloured-dots way either.

The Blair Witch Project presents this conundrum through Heather's obsession with filming everything she can. Mike and Josh are constantly telling her to put the camera down, until at a crucial point in the movie Josh turns the lens on Heather and says, "I realize why you like this camera so much. It's not quite reality."

While the camera has a distancing effect, as a barrier between a human face and the present moment it's archiving, it also causes consenting subjects to enter a state of performance. If you know you're being recorded, you know that somewhere else in time you are being watched. It could be by anyone, at any period in the future. The camera becomes a window to the audient void, and we put our best face forward. We perform who we think we are and we act how we think we'd act in the situation we're in. We self-censor, panopticon style. It's like the Heisenberg uncertainty principle, but for identity.

In the nineties, the pinnacle of this performed identity conundrum was *The Real World*, so naturally the climactic moment in *The Blair Witch Project* uses reality TV shorthand to illustrate Heather's desperation for her life to be fiction. She turns the camera on herself, à la reality show confession booth, and pours all her emotions into that terrible film machine. She performs to beckon the audient void, attempting to fill her lonely terror, and in turn disappears into the affectations of how one should act when fear-stricken on tape.

—

Found footage values audience interpretation above authorial intent. A dead documentarian can't attend her own post-screening Q&A.

—

More people have seen video theories about what *Petscop* might mean than have watched the actual found footage. My favourite theory is by a YouTuber named MatPat, who posits that *Petscop* is a training algorithm for some kind of terrible AI intended to rebirth dead children. His videos have between three and ten million views each. Meanwhile, the first entry in *Petscop* has half that, a viewership that diminishes over the course of the following twenty-four episodes, with the average balancing out at about 600,000 plays.

It's depressing that explainer videos about a piece of art so singular and conceptually successful as *Petscop* are so much more popular than the primary text. But this is how found footage works. The incomplete fragmentary narrative, the lack of an author, the weird effect performance has on identity—all of these strange annihilations combine to create a vacuum that sucks us into the authorial void. We become meta-scribes in the absence of an artist statement. Reading about *Petscop* on Reddit, or watching theory videos forwarding a specific reading of the disturbing footage, it's all part of the *Petscop* experience. In this way, MatPat is a co-author. In another way, so am I.

—

Am I writing *Petscop* right now? Are you reading *Petscop*?

"We are born in terror and trembling," writes theatre direc-tor Anne Bogart in her essay "Terror," from her collection *A Director Prepares.* "In the face of our terror before the uncon-trollable chaos of the universe, we label as much as we can with language in the hope that once we have named some-thing, we need no longer fear it. This labelling enables us to feel safer but also kills the mystery in what has been labelled, removing the life and danger from what has been defined."

In pointing to *Petscop*, have I doomed us to languish in the gravity of voracious art as we attempt to label the unde-finable? Can true horror exist only before a question mark?

—

In 2012, I got my first smart phone and my world changed. Suddenly, I could document everything I did, as it happened. I took pictures and videos everywhere I went, sharing them on Instagram and Facebook and Twitter and all those other apps that connected me to all the people who also had smart phones. My friends and I shared our lives passively with each other, one photo caption at a time. Our corporeal space interactions were prefaced by the trail of narrative we laid out with our iPhones and Samsung Galaxies and LG Nexuses. Face to face, we stopped asking questions about each other's days because we'd already seen it. We were experts in each other's lives without trying.

Consumed by my efforts to transition from seemingly never-ending retail and telesales gigs into a sustainable freelance writing career, I could keep tabs on my friends and they could keep tabs on me while I hustled in isola-tion. And I succeeded in my goal, surrounded by pictures of the people I once shared office space with, who I went to school with, who I grew up alongside, as I worked on

Internet content farms from my desk, occasionally interviewing celebrities for blogs, but mostly staying home at my computer, uploading pictures and videos from my phone to social media, keeping everyone informed that I was living a good life and making sure they didn't forget my face.

Eventually, I stopped getting invited to weddings.

—

Are we all just inventions of each other? Are we lost in the converged voids of authorship and audience? Did we all go missing in the proverbial woods outside Burkittsville, Maryland? By interpreting this essay, are you my author? By writing the words you will interpret, am I yours? Hello, creator, it's me, the content.

—

No one's ever been able to record it, but...
   In a ten-storey building, enter an elevator alone.
   Press the button for the fourth floor.
   At the fourth floor, press the button for the second floor.
   At the second floor, press the button for the sixth floor.
   At the sixth floor, press the button for the second floor again.
   At the second floor, press the button for the tenth floor.
   At the tenth floor, press the button for the fifth floor. If a young woman enters the elevator, do not look at her. Do not speak to her. Press the button for the first floor.
   If the elevator ascends to the tenth floor instead, the doors will open to the other world. Leave the woman behind. Do not look at her. The other world will seem the same as our world, but you will be alone and in the dark.

—

There's nothing particularly horrifying about the final footage of Elisa Lam. It's four minutes of security camera footage from the Cecil Hotel (now the Stay on Main) in Los Angeles that depicts the Canadian tourist as she enters an elevator, pushes all the buttons, seems to interact with— and later hide from—a person off-screen. At some point, she pushes all the buttons again. Finally, she exits the frame. It's odd that the elevator door never attempts to close until after her departure, and Lam's erratic behaviour is strange, but mostly the video is just confusing.

The film is famous for its context. It depicts events from January 31, 2013, the day Lam went missing, only to be found on February 19, five days after the LAPD released the footage to the public. Her body was found in the water tower on top of the hotel, naked, floating next to her clothes. The lid to the reservoir was locked from the outside and her body showed no signs of struggle or physical trauma. As the story goes, they only thought to inspect the water tank after hotel guests complained of foul-smelling, discoloured water pouring from their taps.

The Elisa Lam footage is real. The fear around it is real. The events surrounding her death remain unknown. And just as with found-footage fiction, viewers are drawn to the authorial void. Fantasy is injected into the cracks in the narrative, fencing off the edges of unknowable reality with modern folklore. Lam's final captured moments are scary because of how meta-authorship has shaped it.

Lam's death is a black hole hungry for journalists and podcasters, YouTubers and Reddit conspiracy enthusiasts. If you heard about Elisa Lam before now, chances are it was through the framework of true crime or urban legend. *Buzzfeed* sent correspondents to the Stay on Main in a short video summarizing the mystery, kicking off with two young men daring each other to drink the hotel's legendary tap water. The strange-fiction podcast *Tanis* remixed the Cecil Hotel tragedy with the elevator ritual creepypasta, tying knots between pre-existing narrative parallels. All of this content—fiction, non-fiction, commentary, analysis, the book you're holding, the thoughts you're having—contributes to our ongoing collaboration as we attempt to understand how outstanding questions about Elisa Lam's death might fit into the daily theatre of our own lives.

The Stay on Main has only five floors and there's only one world.

—

The camera can't save us. Yes, it can negate, and absorb, and destroy, but it isn't a self-defence weapon. It's a hyperdense tesseract, collapsing time, space, and identity, bringing us all together in a jumbled chaos of memory, context, and perception.

In *Resident Evil 7*, characters, monsters, and deadly situations are introduced to the player through short found-footage sections. The gameplay doesn't shift, nor does your view of events. The only thing that changes is your knowledge that, unlike the main game, this already happened. A reality show cameraman was already burned to death in a *Saw*-esque torture chamber wearing a GoPro, your wife was already abducted by undying swamp people, a contagious bioweapon already leaked out into the bayou where you're trapped. You can see it, you can experience it, you can interpret it. You can learn from it. It can change you. But you can't change what happened. You must feel the terror, give in to the pull of dual voids. You will perform. You will create. And in grotesque sympathy, you will find a type of participation and partnership that defies labelling.

"Out of the almost uncontrollable chaos of life, I could create a place of beauty and a sense of community," says Anne Bogart. "In the most terrible depths of doubt and difficulty, I found encouragement and inspiration in collaborating with others." In the tangle of authorial and audient voids, we make our agony matter. The camera is how we share our pain.

EXTRASENSORY

When I'm carving up a chicken carcass for stock, I can't help but think about Stephen King. Slicing away with my little knife and peeling off the meat, I feel the texture of his most upsetting depictions of mutilation. The auto-cannibalism of "Survivor Type," the hobbling and dismemberment of *Misery*, or worst of all, the gruesome set piece of *Gerald's Game*, wherein a woman handcuffed to a headboard for days in remote wilderness works up the grit to unsheathe her hand from its skin so she can slip out of her bedroom prison. Even the phrase "degloving injury" is enough to make me see stars. I can't help it. Stephen King has gotten to my senses.

For horror to really get under your skin, it needs to be visceral, which is a tall order for stories we consume on the page, the screen, or with our ears. It's easy to see and hear the strange effects of the weird plants growing on Stephen King's character in his segment of the movie *Creepshow*—but to feel the itchiness of it as the green rash spreads up his back, to smell the dankness of his overgrown home, or taste the moss as it spreads across his tongue is not so simple.

The key is a mix of familiarity and the unknown. We don't need to know exactly what it feels like to be degloved; most people know what it's like to have a skin-covered hand, so you're already meeting King halfway. Same goes for the taste of moss growing on our tongues: we're aware of what it feels like to have something fuzzy, or dry, or unpleasant in our mouths. *Creepshow* director George Romero turns up the volume just enough to make you want to scrape your taste buds on your teeth. When I watch a vampire movie, my neck tingles. When I watch *Saw*, I flex my calf muscle. When I read Chuck Palahniuk's short story "Guts"—which culminates in the image of a teenage boy chewing through his prolapsed small intestine after sitting on a pool drain—I literally faint every time.

There's no limit to the extremity of the horrendous sights, sounds, tastes, smells, and feelings the masters of horror can inflict. Even completely invented phenomena—Lovecraft's unfathomable colour out of space, Junji Ito's killer stench from *Gyo*, the deadly unsound from *The Black Tapes Podcast*—are grounded in our corporeal reality. In all their undefinable glory, even the most unthinkable and indescribable extrasensory occurrences fall under the purview of one of five senses.

A feeling is forced into your body and then amplified to an unimaginable extreme. By invoking the grotesque limits of sight, sound, touch, taste, or smell, horror exposes a raw nerve, then scratches it, overloading you with the fear of experiencing unimaginable sensations—being picked apart, carved up, unsheathed, deboned, and boiled. It's pure carnal empathy, knowing the agony of a surrogate body.

I'm thinking of going vegetarian.

ON MADNESS

In H. P. Lovecraft's fictional New England, the only thing separating death from madness is a heartbeat. The nameless narrator in "The Festival" finds this out the hard way. Returning to his hometown of Kingsport, Massachusetts, for a winter solstice celebration, he follows a procession of partygoers into a church and through a trap door down into a subterranean cove that's playing host to a nightmare bacchanal.

On the verge of being driven past the point of insanity by the monsters and cultists he encounters (as well as one of Lovecraft's trademark transdimensional flautists), his only exit blocked by a nightmarish creature, the narrator flings himself into the nearby water in a last-ditch effort to escape. Recovered half-frozen and revived in a local infirmary, he's plagued by the forensic evidence that contradicts his memories of the night. Hospital staff say the footprints he left in the snow suggest he trudged alone to the edge of a cliff and fell into the ocean. He's transferred to Arkham's asylum, St. Mary's Hospital, for better care, little more than a raving corpse.

Madness is a one-way trip in cosmic horror. There's no returning whole once you've experienced the underground coves where things that ought to crawl walk instead, and discoloured flames cast no shadow. You can't unknow the dark enlightenment bestowed upon you under a waning gibbous moon. All you can do is recontextualize your life, accept your new viewpoint, so you can live with the knowledge of your own insignificance. That's why the survivor of

"The Festival" spends the rest of his days in literature's most infamous nuthouse reading the Miskatonic University's copy of *The Necronomicon*. He searches for the words to describe the horrors etched into his brain, memories that defy rational explanation. Only by knowing the names of the unspeakable can he once again anchor himself to a sense of reality, even if it's a darker, truer one than he knew before. Not so he can rejoin normalcy, but so he can stop his horrible freefall of unknowing and rest in peace. Melodramatic, I know, and more than a little metal. But also, in my experience, very relatable.

The old books of magic were written on skin. Virgin leather or parchment harvested from aborted calves supposedly neutralized the powerful words written on them, cleansing any impure intentions held by the author. Ancient grimoires contained the names of demons, the domains they lorded over, how to call them forth and, most importantly, instructions on how to dispel them. Hidden words and symbols granted the reader control over Agchonion, the dirty spectral swine spreading mischief in the swaddling clothes of infants, or Autothith, the abhorrent lord of grudges conjuring arguments between friends.

    I didn't know the names of the demons plaguing me as I sat on a couch in an empty condo, shirtless and drunk on red wine, fiddling with a plastic triple-action shaving cartridge. But I aimed to discover them. The plan: loosen a piece of sharp metal and mark my naked side with two asterisks to commemorate the gunshot wounds on my father's chest. Three months had passed since I'd seen him shot in that failed mugging, since I'd carried him through a Costa Rican morning to safety, since I'd survived and he'd survived and everything turned out fine. Three more days of grand debauchery aboard a Carnival cruise was my reward, an ocean-bound solstice festival indifferent to my experience, cold like the Toronto December that had awaited me back home. Now the ghost of the bullet that pierced Dad's chest would mark me. Finally, I'd have carnal proof that my story didn't end at survival.

Twisting the shaving cartridge didn't work. Neither did my attempts to uncap it by digging my fingernails into a seam. I tried bending it and wiggling the casing back and forth. I'd never cut myself before. I didn't know where to get real razor blades. But I needed to make my anguish tangible, if not by naming it, then by creating the sacred geometry of fake entry and exit wounds.

I heard a click. The blue-and-grey plastic flew across the room, landing in a corner near the window. My left thumb burned with the sting of failure. It bled. The pain boiled, evaporating into frustration that filled me with doubt. I washed and bandaged my thumb, put the unbroken cartridge back in the travel shaving kit under the bathroom sink, and retired to my bedroom. I screamed and cried and writhed that night, wishing I had the words to describe the terrible thing inside my core that drove me to attempt such a grisly form of self-expression. The language remained occulted. My longing to speak hidden names remained.

There's a place between sanity and insanity, between definitive answers. In that place, unmoored from natural law and expectation, the present moment is overwhelmed with infinite possibility. You become adrift. The trigger—an underground Lovecraftian monster party, for instance—is an experience that can't be ignored and contradicts the rules by which we comprehend the universe. What's left is a choice: either the remarkable things you see and feel are figments of your imagination, and your divergent experience is simply invalid, or you're right and everyone else is wrong.

Psychological horror aspires to conjure this drifting state and sustain it with unreliable narrators and uncanny creep-outs. Once the titular monster in the 2014 movie *The Babadook* introduces itself via a threatening children's pop-up book that mysteriously appears in Amelia's home, the tortured single mother is caught between unbridled imagination and uncharted reality. The Babadook is either a hostile entity with a desire to kill her son or it's a hallucinatory symptom of the stress that comes from surviving a fatal car crash that left her the sole guardian of a boy who builds weapons as a hobby and screams *all the time*. As an audience, we are never given answers, only conflicting hints concerning the true nature of the title monster.

To us, the space between those two paradigms is entertaining. But for Amelia, the stakes feel extremely high. If she decides to not believe in a scary, child-killing monster and turns out to be wrong, her kid will be murdered by the Babadook. And as frightening as the irrational alternative is—accepting that we live in a world that contains a Babadook—at least she's acknowledging the threat. It feels paranormal. It feels insane. But regardless of its tangible nature, the Babadook represents something that's happening to and around Amelia.

By the end of the film, accepting the presence of the Babadook allows Amelia to appease it. She locks the beast in her basement, feeding it bowls of earthworms, and it lingers there, benign. The monster's shape, the sounds it makes, and every terrible feeling it inspires can be contained because she's accepted it as valid to her own experience. The physical reality of the Babadook doesn't matter, and neither does Amelia's sanity. The important thing is to face a fear and accept it honestly. Forbearance can't cure madness, but it can restore balance, and that's often enough to keep someone alive.

Talking is supposed to help. That's the common advice, and it's so ubiquitous I once heard it spoken over the PA system of a black-lit Vancouver bowling alley, eight years into the post-traumatic period of my life. In between nineties pop hits and seventies cosmobowl staples like "Disco Inferno" played a short recording: "There are no known cures for post-traumatic stress disorder, but talking about it helps," repeated a calm woman, like some kind of DJ crisis-line operator.

Her voice electrified something inside me. I knew she was right, but it wasn't so easy. Talking through trauma with my cognitive behavioural therapist gave me the tools to avoid relapses into drunken episodes of attempted skincraft and to better deal with my flashbacks, hypervigilance, and avoidance. But talking was a symptom of its own. It felt like a shell-shocked cliché to scream at the ceiling-mounted speaker near the vending machine, "You don't know how hard that is!" So I bowled in silence.

I can feel the raving impulse long before it blooms. Like all my symptoms, it begins with a memory and a slow-building pressure in my diaphragm. But, unlike the sensory overload of PTSD's other manifestations, raving is harder to hide. Tension builds in my arms and chest over the course of hours, maybe days, and I catch myself muttering small bits of personal narrative under my breath. Eventually, I inject allusions to my traumatic past into conversations and social media posts. And finally, when the tension reaches its breaking point, I find a person who doesn't know my story and begin to jabber like a madman.

On dates in restaurants, in rehearsal studios with theatre creators, in the managers' offices of my customer service and telemarketing jobs, my audience always says the same thing: "You don't have to talk about it if you don't want to."

But I have to.

I try to mask my lack of control. Once the gibbering starts, however, the past overtakes me like a wave. "It all happened in 2006," I say. "My parents took my brother and me on a Caribbean cruise."

I ramble about the context, detailing minor family conflicts surrounding the vacation and explaining how cruises work by taking sweaty hedonists to various ports and spiriting them away on daylong tours. Kayaking, mountain climbing, rum drinking, swimming with dolphins.

"On December 27, we visited Costa Rica," I say. "My mom and brother went on a zip-lining excursion, and my dad and I went on a self-guided walking tour of the port town, which ended with us on a wooden pier near the municipal hall, looking out over the ocean. That's where it happened."

I stop for a moment. I breathe. I can't believe I'm doing this again.

"Don't worry," I say. "No matter how dire this starts to sound, everything turns out fine."

"You don't have to keep going if you don't want to."

But I do.

"A man intercepted us as we tried to leave the pier. His eyes were wide and scared. He showed us a gun—a baby blue .38 snub nose. I thought it looked just like a toy. I thought maybe it wasn't even real. Maybe he was bluffing. He asked us for money. We'd left it all on the ship. He asked again, jabbing the pistol in my direction. Dad snapped. He kicked at the stranger. Twice. Which probably sounds really bizarre, but if you knew him, it wouldn't. Then—pop. The shot sounded like a small firework. My dad crumpled to the ground and the stranger ran off."

When I'm raving, half my vision is there on the pier. The other half is making aggressive eye contact with my audience, desperately clinging to present reality. My breath is collarbone shallow. Self-conscious about oversharing, I skip details of the walk back: the number of times I dropped my bleeding father; the part where, leaving him in a pile on the street, I run back to the crime scene to retrieve the broken shoe that fell off his foot; the weird tug-of-war I played with paramedics over my unconscious dad's body, fearful that if they took him away I'd never see him again. I usually just say, "I had to carry him back to the ship. It was a long walk. And then the medical officer fixed him up. We went on a tour of the judicial system. They never found the gunman because in the police lineup I picked the fourth guy and Dad picked another man wearing a camouflage jacket. The whole thing was over before my mom and brother came back from their excursion. Our vacation went on like nothing ever happened. Everything turned out fine."

And then it's done. My pulse thumps in my ears. I feel humiliated, naked, and, worst of all, unsatisfied. No matter how many times I run though my five minutes of cold reportage, I never communicate what I want to. It took me years to realize I was telling the wrong kind of story. I couldn't feel the release of expression because I was speaking the wrong language.

I raved because I misframed my personal narrative as a story of trauma—a story of adventure. Stories use conflict as their fuel and therefore must subject their characters to trauma, be it emotional, physical, spiritual, or otherwise. The traumatic experience is a story with a strong, tangible conflict.

The post-traumatic experience, on the other hand, is fuelled by the friction between the tangible present reality and memory. It's a conflict between a body and the phantoms of past experience, challenging our natural inclinations for closure. The post-traumatic experience is the stuff of horror, and so it requires a language befitting that genre.

My obsession with horror sprouted naturally from my PTSD. After therapy helped me get my violent and depressive ideation under control, I discovered that frightening and pessimistic entertainment was cathartic. Scary video games simulated minor hypervigilance symptoms, venting my built-up nervous energy. Scary movies gave me something else to have nightmares about. My raving was addressed by reading scary stories.

In the pages of H. P. Lovecraft, I found protagonists who survived otherworldly terror only to end up mentally maimed. The narrators in Lovecraft's "Dagon" and "The Festival" are survivors of adventure, but the shadows of their experiences still haunt them—whether it's in the form of a slimy hand at the window or the terrible memory of a hedonistic subterranean tentacle party. Like me, the Lovecraftian protagonist lives in a permanent personal epilogue where technically everything turns out fine, but nothing feels right, so they are compelled to obsess over their past trauma in a dark present tense.

I consumed cosmic horror the way an optimist gobbles up self-help books. It gave me the eldritch linguistic knowledge to reframe my personal history from traumatic to post-traumatic, from adventure to horror. And that's when I started writing about it. In the absence of *The Necronomicon*, I became the author of my own demon codex.

First, I collected and compiled. I dug out stacks of old notebooks, theatre-history lecture notes written in spiral-bound Hilroys, first drafts of monologues on memo pads, constructive criticism for my classmates' performances written on the back of photocopied scripts for projects I was assistant directing—each of these was a stepping stone back to those early days when the monsters were new and I couldn't help but bring them to life in the margins. Other texts piled on too: the red hardcover journal I kept for every day of the cruise, my cabin key card, the carbon copy of the police report marked with my jagged, adrenaline-drenched signature. I transported myself into my younger mind so I could look into my worst pain and label it.

I burrowed into the shale of paper and violence and where I found a monster I named it. Using the tools and language of horror, I shaped my afflictions into beasts and abominations. For what I couldn't describe, well, horror had me covered there too. Was something unspeakable? Unthinkable? Untypeable? If it worked for the likes of the unknowable Great Old Ones, then it would work for me too. For the spectral image of the gunman, I called him Number 4—a name recovered from the text of a one-act play I wrote when I was twenty-two and raving into my word processor—and he became a manifestation of my own personal Nyarlathotep, Lovecraft's Crawling Chaos. My collapsing nausea and compulsion to writhe on the ground in mental agony: those were the effects of a terrible bleeding red nucleus that pulsed in my core with a sick gravity, like an inner-space version of William Hope Hodgson's evil stars. The bone-white cruise ship that loomed over my bad dreams: it was both a place and a fiend. It was my floating Overlook Hotel with a twenty-four-hour buffet. It was a great idiot god of perverted ceremony, revelling in the constant demented tune of Jimmy Buffett, its mad piper.

Writing everything out chronologically as a horror narrative, I found never-before-acknowledged parts of my life reflected in the compiled manuscript. My *Post-Traumanomicon* validated the existence of malevolent forces that plagued me for years in silence, twisting my bones and devouring my sleep. I finished the book in Halifax, where cruise ships visit in the summer, horns bellowing to announce their arrival, summoning Number 4, igniting the red nucleus, cueing up my nightmares. But my tome of mental anguish, while it never banished these abominations, did something just as important: it proved to me my torment was real.

My grimoire isn't made of skin. It's spread throughout notebooks and across servers. It's ink on paper, it's a PDF, it's a collection of blog posts and emails. Like the narrator from "The Festival," I had a book of names to contextualize my terrible memories and sensations rooted in a winter solstice celebration that went all Cthulhu on me. Like Amelia, I had a basement for my Babadook. The effects of my trauma, tangible thanks to the language of horror, finally existed outside my aching, traumatized body. With my narrative reshaped and a glossary of terms to express it, I learned to live while haunted, to navigate the drifting darkness as I belayed myself to strange explanations. I decided to stop raving and live with monsters.

CANNIBAL SYMPOSIUM

"Does anybody mind if we ask for nachos with no meat?"

It's one of those sweltering afternoons you get in Toronto around June when sidewalks radiate heat lines like stone ovens. The writer sits with the editor and the sales rep on a rooftop bar patio, trying not to fry.

"I always forget you're a vegetarian," says the editor.

The writer pours his colleagues each a glass of beer from the pitcher in the middle of the table before serving himself. The three clink glasses.

"To a meeting of the minds," says the sales rep.

"So, I got into an argument the other day," says the writer, "and I want to get your opinions on something. It's about a cannibal. A long time ago, a German computer repairman sent out personal ads looking for someone he could kill and then eat. And he went through all this trouble to vet each candidate, make sure they knew he was serious, and get their consent. Eventually, he got a guy—a computer engineer—who recorded a video confession proving he was totally fine with being slaughtered and consumed. So, the night comes and the engineer drinks a bunch of wine and takes a bunch of sleeping pills, and they amputate his penis. And I guess they fry it? They cook it with herbs and garlic, and they eat it together. Then the engineer goes into the bathtub and the repairman kills him for good, then puts the body on meat hooks and continues to eat him for a period of time."

"I've heard about this," says the editor. "There's a Rammstein song about it."

The server arrives, and the writer orders vegetarian nachos. Then he continues: "The cannibal repairman was caught and convicted of manslaughter, but was retried a few years later and ended up with a murder conviction. Do you think that's the right charge? Because I'm not so convinced."

Sales shakes her head. "It's murder at the very least, but the repairman also mutilated the victim while he was alive. There's a whole subplot in *Hannibal* where Mads Mikelsen feeds Eddie Izzard to himself and it's way worse than regular murder."

"No way," says the editor. "If he's got to be charged, it's manslaughter. But I'm not sure what he did was a crime at all. It was fully consensual. And if suicide isn't a criminal act, then the same should go for euthanasia. The penis thing is just an extreme sexual act between two consenting adults. And otherwise, the engineer was dead, right? He was just an object. If the repairman is guilty of anything, it's not being thorough enough about permits for euthanizing someone. And there's body disposal regulations he definitely violated. At worst, this is a case of poaching."

"That's a more extreme take than I expected," says the writer. "Very libertarian."

"I just don't want to kink-shame anyone or tell them how to die."

"You aren't taking this seriously," says the sales rep. "This isn't about kink-shaming. This is about a taboo shared by all animals and societies for all of time. You don't eat your own. Honestly, I'm surprised there isn't an actual law explicitly against cannibalism."

"There are anti-desecration laws that would technically cover this," says the writer. "I looked into it. But, in Canada at least, they only carry up to five years' imprisonment."

"That law needs to be amended," says sales.

"I guess I can see it from both sides," says the writer. "It's abhorrent, but we shouldn't overcriminalize abhorrence. That's a slippery slope."

"Is it?" asks sales. "I think that's a pretty reasonable line to draw: don't eat human meat."

"But you and I know from experience that has religious implications," says the editor. "We both went to Catholic school, we've both done communion. That's ritual cannibalism."

"That's eating bread!"

"Not to true believers it isn't. Aside from the sexual element of the Rammstein case, the engineer is basically a Christ figure, since Jesus was also consensually killed and subsequently eaten."

"I'm no Catholic, so correct me if I'm wrong, but Jesus is God, right? So that's maybe a technicality. There's magic involved."

The server returns, placing the plate of nachos in the centre of the table. The three are silent for a moment.

"Would you do it, though?" asks the editor. "Would you eat human meat? There's that start-up that everyone was talking about a few years ago—thinking of it now, maybe it was a hoax—but there was that start-up that wanted to sell lab-grown salami made from cultivated Kanye West. Would you eat the Kanye West sausage?"

"I might try it," says the writer. "For the experience."

The sales rep taps away at her phone.

"Ew," says the editor. "Why?"

"Well, I'm a vegetarian, but the prospect of lab-grown meat is appealing to me. There's no suffering involved; it's cultivated and grown and harvested. Basically, it's a plant. No central nervous system, no consciousness."

"I looked it up," says sales. "BiteLabs. They want to make salami out of Kanye, and Ellen, and J-Law, and James Franco. Apparently they're serious, but they don't have willing participants. Their meat is thirty percent celebrity. I'd eat James Franco meat."

The editor balks. "How is this better than the German thing? It's consensual, it's human meat. Is it because they're still alive? Because for me that makes it worse. It's a lot more intimate. What's the difference between eating Kanye salami and eating his snot? It's human by-product. That's disgusting."

"Fascinating you mention the intimacy," says the writer. "The biggest issue I see is that I don't feel like these celebrities match my cultural taste. I don't listen to Kanye. Franco's annoying. Ellen seems like a hypocrite to me, and I'm a bit meh on Lawrence. Not to mention the gender implications of eating women. I'm not a monster. Now, if they made meat out of Sam Mendes..."

"The director of *American Beauty*?" The editor drops a salsa-loaded chip onto the wooden table. "Fuck."

"Yeah," says the writer. "I really like Mendes. I'd eat Mendes."

"So, you'd eat lab-grown human if we put them on these nachos?" asks the sales rep.

"Yes. If it was Sam Mendes. Or Werner Herzog."

"Herzog is a good one," says sales.

"I can't believe the tables turned against me here," says the editor. "How am I the prude now?"

"Life comes at you fast," says sales.

"Okay," says the editor. "Now I'm feeling self-conscious. You wouldn't eat actual human product but you would eat by-product? Am I getting that right? Is there any scenario where you'd do real cannibalism?"

"In a plane crash," says sales. "In an *Alive* situation."

"Oh—here's a hypothetical then," says the writer. "In an *Alive* scenario, what do you eat first? How do you cook it? I'd eat the meat to survive, but I don't think I could prepare it myself, honestly. I'd need it to be presented to me in an obscure manner."

"I don't know a ton about cuts of meat," says the editor, "but I feel like there's a correct answer to this and that answer is the rump. You roast it over the fire."

"On this, we agree," says sales. "You gotta eat the butt."

"That was easy," says the writer.

The server checks on the table. The trio order another pitcher of beer.

"I have to say," says the editor, "all this public talk about cannibalism makes me nervous. I was half-expecting our server to ghost us. The last thing I want is to end up like that cannibal cop from New York."

"What cannibal cop?" asks the sales rep, already typing into her phone.

"This guy who worked for the NYPD and his wife found all these Internet role-playing transcripts that seemed to suggest he had fantasies of kidnapping her, killing her, and eating her," says the editor. "I know he went to trial."

"Gilberto Valle," says sales, reading from her phone. "According to Google, he was convicted for conspiracy to kidnap but was acquitted."

"So that guy is free, but the German cannibal is in prison?" asks the editor. "I get it, but also, what the fuck?"

The writer pours the beers. "It's a free speech issue, isn't it? Valle didn't do anything. He had disturbing thoughts, but shouldn't there be space to have those kinds of thoughts? It's not like we should be prosecuted for having this conversation."

"But to me, Valle is more dangerous than the repairman," says the editor. "His fantasies were nonconsensual. The repairman went out of his way to get consent. When it comes down to which type of cannibal I'd rather have living in my neighbourhood, I'm picking the one who can take no for an answer."

"But the cop didn't do anything!" says the writer.

"I want them both locked up," says the sales rep. "I want a cannibal-free society. There needs to be a limit to our liberal acceptance. This is it. We found it. Congrats."

"Maybe a registry would work," says the editor. "But even then, I just am not scared of a guy like the repairman. I empathize too much with the engineer. I really understand sometimes wanting to die."

They laugh in agreement. Glasses clink once again, this time in an ironic toast led by the writer—"Eat the rich!"—and the conversation turns to rising rent prices.

WALLPAPER

Nurikabe is a yokai, a monster from Japanese folklore. Traditionally depicted as a giant, flabby, three-eyed dog, the beast's broad side acted like a mobile wall. At night, Nurikabe was blamed for getting in the way of strolling humans, especially drunk ones, misdirecting them, guiding them away from their destinations, getting them lost. Nurikabe's victims ended up in different towns, different homes, woke up in strange beds—pranked by a spectral pup, led astray by a ghost dog. But that's not how we know Nurikabe now. Today, thanks to yokai expert Shigeru Mizuki's children's horror manga *GeGeGe no Kitaro*, Nurikabe survives in modern stories as a walking wall with tired eyes. It's a dramatic revision, but Mizuki was the authority on yokai. He encountered one, after all.

The Japanese manga artist, folklorist, historian, and children's horror author laid the foundations for some of the most popular cultural phenomena of this millennium. If not for Mizuki's art, yokai would have been lost to obscurity, and without yokai to serve as their inspiration, there would be no Pokémon—which seems like an odd hook on which to hang modern pop culture until you consider Pikachu was once more recognized globally than Mickey Mouse.

A left-handed visual artist, Shigeru Mizuki endured a storied life of close calls, strange escapades, and suffering, all of which he chronicled in a series of visual memoirs. He was conscripted into the Japanese army during World War II and went on to survive an Imperial suicide order, a chronic malaria infection, the ingestion of human feces, and an explosion that claimed his drawing arm. But all of that pales in comparison to one particularly uncanny close call detailed in his historical memoir *Showa*.

One day, when Muzuki was stationed in Papua New Guinea, before the bombing that would claim his limb, his barracks came under fire. He fled into the jungle. Under enemy pursuit, he took to the ocean and spent hours stealthily treading water, swimming cove to cove, looking for a safe place to come ashore. Finally back on land, he was spooked by indigenous Papuans and fled back into the night.

Mizuki was lost. Groping his way through the brush, he came to a point where he could walk no farther. His progress was prevented by "an invisible wall," as he describes it in *Showa*. So he slept where he stopped. Upon waking, Mizuki expected to see a wall. Instead, he found a sheer cliff drop. He'd been saved by a yokai.

"If it weren't for Nurikabe," Mizuki wrote, "I would have walked into the darkness and died."

But, of course, that's crazy talk. Not to besmirch the dead, but walking wall creatures don't save soldiers' lives. Nurikabe doesn't even exist.

Belief in the paranormal has a stigma. I should know; I've never encountered a yokai but I used to pray to angels. In my childhood bedroom, at night before karate tournaments, I gripped the red bohemian crystal beads comprising my chaplet of Saint Michael and recited obscure Catholic oaths directed at the celestial choirs. I wanted the heavenly beings to descend into the ring and imbue my punches and kicks with divine power, to turn my opponents into pillars of salt, Old Testament style. It never worked, and I kept my weird nighttime wishes of mystical power a secret. Even though we were taught in school that angels and saints were real, a shameful miasma emitted from the practical application of our more mystical lessons.

The shame is similar to telling a ghost story to a skeptic—the kind where you have to admit up front that what you're about to say doesn't make sense. "I know this is going to sound strange," you might say, "but after my granddad died, I started being visited by a shadowy figure at night." Or maybe: "I don't believe in ghosts, but when I used the Ouija board I found in my dead oma's attic, a spirit claimed to be her." Unless it's a conventional tenet of a mainstream religion, we're only allowed to believe in the extrasensory within the bounds of humiliation. We have to apologize before making a ridiculous claim, so we say things like, "I can't be right about this, because it can't happen, but a yokai saved my life."

Before I believed in angels, I believed in ghosts that lived in my bedroom walls. I believed in the trolls my cousin Jordan said roamed the forests around the Rideau Lakes, turning children into wooden statuettes to decorate their caves. After I stopped believing in angels, I still believed in God. Then I believed in the prescriptivist popular science of new atheism, and after that I believed in string theory, with all its multiversal elegance, unprovability, and parallels with the Christian mysticism I've always yearned to replicate. I believed in nothing too—that real nihilism where you don't even care to try suicide because there's no difference between life and death. And after a few decades of searching, looking back on my journey to find a faith that fits, I can say with confidence: despite their conflicting aesthetics, every spiritual paradigm I tried on fulfilled the same role. All I've ever wanted was an explanation for the chaos of life.

A genre isn't a faith, but, as a set of conventions and archetypes, it can help us understand faith's role in our personal narratives. In this way, horror can liberate us from the shame of trying on different existential frameworks to see what fits. It can give us the tools to respect our experiences. Horror suggests there isn't an objective metaphysics we can know as humans. It posits belief as decentralized, that all spooky stories, no matter how conflicting, are legitimate. You don't need to believe in yokai to accept Shigeru Mizuki's life-saving encounter. Each life is a haunted house with its own wallpaper—full of ghosts, goblins, angels, and giant trickster dogs—that keeps us from wandering into darkness.

DEVIL'S NOSTRIL

Sometimes I forget Satan is supposed to be the bad guy. After seeing *The Witch*, a 2015 period drama set in 1630 that ends with its protagonist, Thomasin, signing the Devil's book and joining a coven of naked women in the woods, I thought, *Good for her*. The next day, on my work's Slack channel, I recommended the movie to my friend Alex, telling him I found it inspiring. But when he watched *The Witch*, all he saw was horror.

"How is that inspiring? Her family died and she sold her soul to the Devil."

He had a point. That's Satan's whole deal: sucking up souls to keep them away from the abstract bliss of Heaven and Jesus's eternal love. But still, as Thomasin joins her weird sisters around a bonfire in the forest, she begins to float with them, and, counter to the nightmare chorus scoring the scene, she smiles—and so do I.

"Don't you see the liberty of the scene?" I asked. "The whole movie, Thomasin is mistreated in the name of a puritanical God who is wholly absent in her life. Then, after all her suffering, she's finally free."

"She's literally not free. She's enslaved to the Devil."

He had a point. But part of me couldn't come around to understand what was so bad about that. The Devil saved Thomasin from society by connecting her to the world and granting her some small dominion over it. Sure, it's a writhing, naked dominion that requires the occasional human sacrifice under the full moon, but it sure beats the alternative for women in puritanical New England. Maybe I can't help it. Maybe I just like Lucifer.

"Maybe it's a Catholic thing," said Alex, who never once confessed his sins to a priest in a school gymnasium.

He had a point.

Bless me, Father, for I have sinned. It has been four weeks since my last confession. These are my sins: I took the Lord's name in vain, I swore more than a hundred times, I said the F-word, I said the SH-word, I said the A-word and the D-word, I yelled at my mom, I yelled at my dad, I told my mom I hate her, I had angry thoughts, I was greedy, I was selfish, I got in a fight with my brother, I didn't pay attention in church, I didn't want to go to church, I thought about swear words in my head, I told Mark T that nobody liked him and made him cry. For these and all my sins, I am truly sorry.

Sitting on a seafoam-green plastic chair across from Father Mac, I spoke in a guilty mumble, hoping beyond hope he didn't know I was inventing my crimes. My black Kmart sneakers tapped the gymnasium's cement floor. I lied about almost all of it, everything except telling Mark T he was unlikeable, which I genuinely wanted to atone for. That was mean, even if it was accurate. Sometimes telling the truth is the worst kind of sin.

"Why did you say you hate your mom?" asked the priest.

"I just got really angry," I said. But the truth was I hadn't said it. I loved my mom. It was something I heard my younger brother say when she refused to loan him an advance on his allowance so he could buy a new video game. Is it possible to plagiarize a sin? "Also, I took stuff from my brother."

Three Glory Bes, three Our Fathers, four Hail Marys. That's what it took to cleanse my soul of its mostly imagined misdeeds. I joined the other kids at centre court, where a makeshift shrine to Mother Mary sat atop a white sheet on a short table. I knelt, made the sign of the cross, and performed a deep sigh before doubling my penance and muttering the prayers under my breath. When I was done, I opened my eyes and signed the cross, looking at the statue of Mary backdropped by the digital basketball scoreboard mounted on the wall behind her. I so rarely saw that display lit up with actual numbers that I wondered if it even worked.

To me, lying during confession was an anxiety reaction. I was a compulsive rule-follower, but the sacrament of reconciliation assumes the worst. So when the time came to beg forgiveness before God, I felt like I was at the doctor's office needing a prescription for a suddenly asymptomatic illness. The ritual demanded sins, so I paradoxically lied to a priest in order to play my role, gambling that God would take the extra penance I assigned myself as payment for my fraudulent bill. You could say I was neurotic for a preteen, but mostly I just didn't want to be tortured for all eternity in the furnaces of Hell.

My motivation to be good was completely negative. I didn't really know anything about Heaven, certainly not enough to want to go there. But for as long as I can remember, I've had a vivid picture of Hell as a red subterranean cave with pools of glowing molten rock and giant orange flames that dance to the screams of souls in agony. When you die and go to Hell, you still have a body, so it can be torn apart slowly by lesser demons, so it can be shoved into a small dark box lined with nails and broken glass, so it can be regenerated just to be flayed all over again. Hell makes you thirsty. Hell makes you realize that little extra effort to be good when you were alive would have been worth it. Hell is very easy to conceptualize and even easier to go to.

My teachers always said the worst part about Hell is the absence of God, but since my knowledge of the afterlife was so one-sided, I naturally used that same logic to understand Heaven. Heaven was good because it wasn't Hell. And that was pretty much all I knew about it. I had a vague idea of judgment, my dead grandparents, and the cliché image of St. Peter at the gates to let people in, but other than that, I couldn't really appreciate Heaven as a reward. I didn't know what to expect, which scared me. The conundrum made death into a high-stakes trick question: would you rather go to the familiar image of Hell in your head or someplace you know absolutely nothing about?

I could have used a pen pal like the anonymous monk who authored *The Cloud of Unknowing*, a fourteenth-century mystic text about the inability to comprehend God in Heaven. Structured as a series of letters to a young Christian acolyte, *The Cloud of Unknowing* describes a type of prayer called contemplation through which a worshipper can come to have an audience with the divine, first by passing through a cloud of forgetting and then through the titular nullifying fog, finally entering a pure state of egoless reception with the godhead. The inability to know God through our senses is the crux of Anonymous Monk's practice, but he understands the Holy darkness of forgetting one's eyes as bliss.

Still, the contemplative monk fell into the same trap as I did. His Christian grimoire is constantly occupied with the unknowability of God in Heaven. But when it comes to the Devil, no detail is spared. Anonymous writes:

"...I've learned from students of necromancy, who conjure evil spirits, from those to whom the devil has appeared in physical form, that when he assumes human shape, he only has one nostril, and it is flat and wide. And he's always willing to flare it up at people so they can get a good look at his brain, which is nothing but the fire of hell, and he likes nothing better than convincing people to look up there, because when they see it, they lose their minds forever."

The symbols of Hell are stronger than the icons of Heaven because the culture of Christianity permits us to recognize them (as long as we don't worship them). The punishment of Hell hinges on our ability to understand it at least partially as a corporeal sensory experience, and as a torture we deserve. We have to regret breaking the Ten Commandments to contextualize the torture. So there's no need to pass through clouds of forgetting and unknowing to contemplate the Devil's playground. We are free to imagine Satan, to paint pictures of his realm and write poems about his sadness. It comes naturally. And that's why it was so upsetting when the Pope abolished Hell.

"There's no such thing as Hell," said Mrs. G, my Grade 10 religion class teacher. "The Vatican says when St. Michael the Archangel defeated Lucifer, the Devil was banished to Earth. That's why he is able to tempt us."

I'm not entirely sure of the veracity of this, since being raised Catholic means coming to terms with many layers of mythology, authority, and guilt, but it sounded on brand. Hell on Earth is easy to believe in when you're a teenager with undiagnosed bipolar II sitting in high school religion class. Of course, metaphysics aside, the problem with a Hell that we already inhabit is that it makes the afterlife wholly unimaginable. And, as we know from Lovecraft, the greatest horror is that which we cannot comprehend.

"In death," said Mrs. G, "we have a chance to make penance. We are made to pray in purgatory until we are saved."

"What about Hitler?" shouted my surly friend Josh, buzzed on the rum-spiked milkshakes he'd smuggled into class. Religion was a tougher school subject for some of us than for others.

Mrs. T squirmed.

"If, in purgatory, Hitler accepts Christ's love and undergoes the transformation of reconciliation and penance, then yes," she said. "As Catholics, we believe all can be redeemed. Even Hitler can go to Heaven."

That didn't seem right. But then again, who was I to say? The rules were all laid out, and eternity is a long time to ask for forgiveness. Still, it seemed like Heaven, the unknowable metaphysical space that would hypothetically forgive genocide, was becoming even less appealing: a vague place you go when you die, as long as you're good, and Hitler might be there. Great.

I always expected I'd go back to church after I moved away from home. But Toronto's churches seemed inaccessible to me by virtue of the city's size, and my university didn't have any mandatory religion classes or school-wide gatherings for Catholic mass. In the back of my head, I planned to do confession for my absence, and make like the prodigal son in a hey-Father-sorry-I-haven't-called sort of way.

Easter was approaching, the big holiday marking Jesus's resurrection. Arriving at my apartment after a day of rehearsals, I found a phone message from my high school friend Laura.

"Hi, Peter, I hope you're enjoying being a big-time actor. I have some bad news, so get ready. I was just back home and Liz told me Josh died. I know you two were friends so I wanted to let you know. I think it was a car crash."

It wasn't.

I returned home for the funeral, where I sat in a wooden church pew next to the one close friend I shared with Josh.

Surrounded by the faculty from my Catholic school, in front of a big black-and-white picture of my old pal's face, the truth came out. He had jumped off a bridge.

One of the eulogies cited his suicide note, saying he had trouble squaring the problem of evil with the existence of an all-loving and all-powerful God. At least, that was my take-away.

I didn't stop believing that spring afternoon, but I never went back to church. When I returned to Toronto, I sat on my bed and listened to *Lateralus*, a metal record I associated with Josh, and cried for a very long time, trying to imagine Heaven but failing to contemplate the opposite of Earthly pain.

Singing is ten times more powerful than prayer, according to the divine calculus they taught me in elementary school. Week after week, the same gymnasium where I gave confession was transformed into a makeshift Catholic church where three hundred students sat on rows of those seafoam-green stackable chairs. Father Mac intoned the liturgy and the homily, and gave communion, which even as children we knew to be the flesh of an ancient man-god. A complicit, people-eating student body. When it came time in the sermon for a hymn, we all opened duotangs to lyrics printed on copy paper and recited rock songs, slightly altered to reflect the manifest destiny of the school—most notably, John Lennon's "Imagine" with the modified line "and *one* religion too."

I ate up the singing-prayer math like it was a second host wafer. Singing is louder and more attractive than whispered, shameful devotions. Joining in with the flock of my peers was the perfect way to ensure God saw me. If he noticed me there, putting all I had into the "oo-ooo-oo-oooo" right before the chorus of my school's Christian remix of "Imagine," I was sure to add one more point to the list of reasons I wouldn't be going to Hell.

I didn't commit my last sin, apostasy, until after I graduated from Catholic school. At age nineteen, my transition into a faithless heathen was complete. But that divine scoring system still hangs over my head, like a phantom appendage, and aches with guilt whenever I have bad thoughts. God's disappointed gaze, like the spectral eyes of a parent I killed, burns into the emotional core I used to call a soul. Like the dog who used to belong to an abusive owner, I keep bracing for God's rolled-up Sunday edition to pop me on the spiritual nose. To shake these dreadful feelings, I turn to music.

My favourite tune for getting the fear of God off my back is "He Is" from *Meliora* by the Swedish metal band Ghost. The song is an anti-hymn that defies the group's genre categorization. The delicate guitar picking of the song's verses, the rapturous vocals, the repetition of the song title, everything except the guitar solo makes "He Is" sound like the kind of song I'd find in that duotang gym hymnal from my childhood. But when I listen to the lyrics, there is no mistaking "He Is" for anything else. It's as metal as music gets, literally Devil worship.

The song's imagery inverts all expectations of holiness conjured by its hymnlike composition. The verses tell of "star-crossed lovers reaching out to a beast with many names," standing next to the abyss, and a world in flames. A lyric in the second verse takes the brightest of Lucifer's pseudonyms, Morningstar, and positions it as a virtuous guide into the void, yearning for annihilation and rejecting the Christian promise of life everlasting. Esoteric, yes, but that only makes the subversion of form all the more insidious as it builds into a God-slaying refrain that positions the Devil as "shining in the light."

The song inverts popular understandings of the divine, flipping a theological trope to inspire a feeling of revelation. A normal hymn would have the Lord shine in the dark, as the Holy Spirit does in the Catholic school staple "Children of the Light." But a bright darkness invokes the unsettling imbalance of divine knowledge exemplified by texts like *The Cloud of Unknowing*. God's light can only be experienced beyond our senses, in a world without eyes or a brain. It's a dark brightness. And because Satan is everything God is not—Earthbound, freedom-loving, knowable—his darkness is one of illumination.

"He Is" is so complete in its blasphemy that it makes me God-fearingly nauseous as I sing along. If a hymn is to thank God for accepting my fealty and the imperfections He built into me, flattering Him for a chance to live forever, then the perfect anti-hymn reverses the value judgment. The perfect anti-hymn turns those faults into virtues, thanking Satan for my flaws and praying for the day I will no longer exist, finally consumed by the abyss, where even God's scrutinizing eye won't find me. Singing along feels sacrilegious, even to me, a non-believer, as I take back all that false penance ten prayers at a time. Maybe it's crazy to deny Heaven on purpose, but at least that insanity is knowable. Get before me, Satan, show me your maddening nostril.

SANTA CLAUS VERSUS THE SMOKE MONSTER

Consider *The Santa Clause*.

It's a horror movie. Really. Divorced toy company executive Scott Calvin accidentally kills Santa by startling him as the jolly old saint tromps around on the roof. Calvin puts on the deceased Claus's clothes and begins to transform. And then, after he saves the Christmas he imperilled, Calvin's body begins to change shape. He doubles in weight, his hair turns shock white, and any attempt to shave his face is met with a full beard regrown mere seconds after his cheeks are smooth.

Calvin is distressed by his transformation. He fights it. He goes to the doctor and worries about his mood swings—from Tim Allenesque misogynist grumpy to revelrous and joyful in an ancient Saturnalian way. His family recognizes him and honours his memory, even as the levee of his consciousness breaks. Calvin is flooded with naughty lists, nice lists, visions of children sleeping and awake, even memories of secrets from decades past: in the final scene he gives Judge Reinhold's character an Oscar Mayer Weenie Whistle, a toy he privately wished for at age three.

By the end of *The Santa Clause*, Scott Calvin no longer resists the creeping metamorphosis because Scott Calvin is dead. He has become host to the Christmas spirit, which holds his knowledge and wears his face.

The moral of the story: don't put on a dead guy's clothes.

Now consider the smoke monster.

Starting in the first episode of the ABC television series *Lost*, the show's ensemble of castaways are terrorized by a sentient black cloud that takes the forms of the dead to lure our protagonists away from safety. It scans their memories and tests their mettle to see who is worth harvesting as an avatar, so it can achieve its goal of escaping its island prison.

In the show's final seasons, the smoke monster takes the form of beloved man of faith John Locke, who died in the fourth season. Locke's return is a false resurrection. The smoke monster attempts to fool everyone on the show (and many viewers at home) that the walking, talking corpse of Locke is really Locke. But he's not.

The smoke monster version of Locke is an abomination. Some preternatural force animates him like a marionette built to scale, vocalizing his catchphrase, regurgitating his memories, manipulating the audience's emotions and those of Locke's living comrades. The grotesque pantomime of the smoke monster in its Locke-suit makes us long for the genuine article taken by the unfairness of death. It presents us with nothing but memory as manipulation, zombie nostalgia. Frankly, it's off-putting, practically offensive.

The moral of the story: memory is not a substitute for reality.

Now consider Louis de Pointe du Lac.

In Anne Rice's *Interview with the Vampire*, Louis describes with longing his transformation into a bloodsucking creature of the night. After drinking the blood of the vampire Lestat, Louis's senses changed. His present moment grew overwhelmingly vibrant. But Louis's new self comes at the price of his living body.

Louis tells the titular interviewer that as soon as he became accustomed to the decadent sights and sounds of vampiredom, his body began to ache: "All my human fluids were being forced out of me. I was dying as a human, yet completely alive as a vampire; and with my awakened senses, I had to preside over the death of my body with a certain discomfort and then, finally, fear."

For Louis, this transformation was literally his death. After centuries of bloodsucking and decadence, Louis came to regret not viewing his passing with reverence and fascination. An eyewitness to his own demise as he was reborn from the outpouring of his fluids, a vessel emptied onto the forest floor, doomed to an eternity of trying to fill himself with the essence of others.

The moral of the story: treat the death of transformation with the reverence you'd give a final sunset.

Finally, consider your cells.

It takes seven years of cellular reproduction for the human body to replace itself completely. By the time you turn seven, the material of your infant self is gone. At fourteen, that seven-year-old is nothing but memories and photographs. At twenty-one, you're barely recognizable, an adult who has moulted three other bodies.

I like to think my transformation is more than a story supported by a narrative of memories, photos, and journal entries. But when I imagine being seven, or fourteen, or twenty-one, I'm really just picturing my present self in another body. I think the way I think now, imposing present values on past scenarios, retrofitting continuity to justify my present politics and cultural taste.

I like to believe that even if the thirty-two-year-old me typing this sentence is borne of four and a half corpses, the shifts have been so gradual as to be painless—nothing like Louis's vampiric birth or Scott Calvin's yuletide possession. But when I think of all the pain those past Peters endured in between the pleasant memories I cling to, I worry as if they were strangers who died without ceremony. I hope the next me remembers the current me with reverence, waking up at age thirty-five and donning my dead man's clothes with at least a bit of sympathy. I hope the next me is more Santa Claus than smoke monster.

I don't know the moral of this story. I expect that's for the next version of myself to figure out. I'm a living memory in the making, destined to serve the aspirations of whoever grows out of my dust. If you're still you when he gets here, can you please ask him for me?

WHEN THE SCREAMING STOPS

Grace survived the night. She'd been through hell. A deadly game of hide-and-seek in which her new in-laws hunted her for sport. That's the plot of 2019's *Ready or Not*, a torturous thrill ride of a movie about different ways to die in a mansion filled with killers. Instead of succumbing, Grace endured. Ripped open against an iron fence, pierced by an arrow, compelled to self-mutilate as a survival mechanism, emotionally wrecked by the betrayal of her newlywed husband, placed on a sacrificial altar like a goat—Grace fucking deserved victory. She was the last girl standing. I sympathized.

Seeing Grace covered head to toe in a full wedding party of blood as the cleansing light of morning blessed her with safety, I felt her catharsis as she destroyed the remainder of her barely late husband's family. I knew this character. She was wearing death. So familiar with the reaper and his myriad methods that amity wasn't even a choice. Her friendship with death was written on her flesh. It stained her wedding dress. Beholding her in this moment of triumph, even just picturing it in my head, I feel my shoulders relax. I feel my anxiety-induced nausea dissipate. I float in the calm that comes with the understanding that life and death are the same phenomenon.

The only blood I've ever been covered in was my dad's, and he's still alive. I emotionally relate to the visual metaphor of a human drenched in viscera and covered in gaping wounds. I'm familiar with the exhaustion of death. I've even seen a digital facsimile of it in *Bloodborne*, a horror video game inspired by the lore of H. P. Lovecraft.

Bloodborne lets you make your own character. In the game, I have my exact shade of red hair. I have my glasses and body frame. I have my nose and chin. And I'm frequently hidden under a thick coat of red-and-black ichor, which is appropriate given the primary mechanic of *Bloodborne* is death. The game is incredibly violent. Your customized character is tasked with navigating "the hunt" in the fictional town of Yarnham—the culling of citizens turned beastly through the side effects of blood transfusions administered as miracle medicine by the local church. Every time you fall in combat against the beasts, which happens a lot because the game is notoriously difficult, you are penalized by having to start over from the beginning.

The game took me three years to complete, and in some play sessions the only progress you make is in your own understanding of the world. You learn how brutal your situation is and that makes you better. Eventually, you don't care about dying. You've done it so much. And you'll do it more too. Much more. When you arrive at the end of the game, your digital doppelgänger drenched in the fluids of bestial things and celestial beings, you will have died to the point where you are better at living than the things that would kill you. There are few experiences in all of entertainment more satisfying.

Every time I play *Bloodborne*, it makes me think of Lake Huron.

When I was a child, my family kept a boat at a marina in Bayfield, a town on Lake Huron that boasts the most beautiful sunset on Earth. The great lake, when it's calm, looks like a mirror, so when the sun descends and the sky catches fire in ribbons of orange, fuchsia, magenta, and midnight blue, it's reflected perfectly, as if two suns are merging and annihilating each other in the scientific sense—matter and antimatter nullifying together. On evenings like this, my dad would drive our boat far out into the water, so far we could barely see land. Surrounded by horizon, we waited for darkness to fall, listening to Dire Straits' *Brothers in Arms*, Pink Floyd's *Wish You Were Here*, and, one summer, a mix CD of Metallica ballads.

Swimming in the deep, always-cold fresh water was my first encounter with the sublime. Floating in something so big and hostile to mammalian life, I'd be a goner if not for the miracle of engineering that got me out there. It was a feeling I wanted to hold on to forever. I wanted to be with the horizon in an infinite twilight, away from life in motion. It feels ridiculous to admit, but my relationship with living has always been wearisome. Sporting dark bags under my eyes since before I could drive, drinking SoBe energy drinks to stay awake on Saturday afternoons, I contemplated ruination casually, with longing, like it was nothing more than an afternoon nap in a luxury coffin. It made me feel less nauseous.

Later, I discovered this Lake Huron aura elsewhere; attending funerals is the social equivalent of surrounding yourself with horizon. Funerals are invigorating. The catharsis of mourning, the pain of grief, the celebration of life remembered, and the regret of opportunities closed off forever. No more time to apologize for that petty conflict, to pay back that long-owed five bucks, to say, "I love you." It's equalizing insomuch as death is ubiquitous. Funerals are a reminder that loss is universal and survival is hard work.

Opa was murdered. While biking alone, he was run off the road by one of those monsters who drive pickup trucks forty above the speed limit and casually joke about killing cyclists. Grandma died of lung cancer. Granddad, her husband, suffered a series of heart attacks while undergoing back surgery. I tried to kill myself and failed, but Josh tried to kill himself and succeeded, and I often wonder about how we were different. My infant cousin died of lung complications. Dad didn't die when he was shot, but I thought he might whenever I dropped him as I tried to drag him to safety. Oma got colon cancer and passed as Mom sat vigil at her bedside. Emma's aunt hanged herself and we adopted her cat, Teddy. Andrew died of lymphoma after holding a theatrical living funeral. Maura died of cancer she hid up until the last moment.

Crying feels good. Funeral voices sound good. Drenched in the temporal viscera of a dozen unspoken eulogies written in my head, sitting in pews and viewing cadavers, proximity to death brings me closer to peace. The way you can feel the ground through the soles of your dress shoes when you gather at the edge of life instead of working or going to school or worrying if people like you—nothing feels better. Funerals are preferable to weddings. I truly believe this. They celebrate something real, non-institutional, and fully inclusive. Death doesn't skip over anyone. If I ever slip up and mention my morbid affinity at a reception, I cover it up with a joke about how I just don't like dancing. But I'd dance at a funeral, if only to celebrate the ghost in the room, our invisible host.

I was a telemarketer when Oma died. I found out about her death while walking to work across Front Street in Toronto; my mom called to tell me. I tried to finish my shift, make my commission, but I broke down in tears on the phone while trying to sell a stranger opera tickets. I left work early and caught a train to Kingston with Nick. Dad picked us up and chauffeured us the rest of the way to Oma's deep, rural, empty home. After the viewing, my right hand chafed from shaking hands with all my grandmother's friends. Dad took me, Nick, and my cousins out for pizza in our suits and dresses. Eating, drinking, easing each other's loss, I remembered Mom's response to me telling her how difficult I was finding telesales: "You should try being a coroner."

Every weekend between Victoria Day and Labour Day, my family drove two hours to the marina where we kept our boat, which we treated like a floating cottage. The road to Bayfield is lined with graveyards, each with its pastoral order of white and grey headstones speckling manicured grass. Back when we were kids (when even Grandma was still kicking), driving by those memorial parks triggered a catchphrase in Nick: "I'm impressed."

No one knows why he developed this affectation. It's just a thing he did. Every time he saw a cemetery, Nick stopped what he was doing—playing Game Gear, reading *Goosebumps*, drawing concept art for a video game he dreamed up—and from the back seat of Dad's grey extended-cab Chevy pickup he'd say it, adding extra emphasis for particularly expansive burying grounds. If my brother was too absorbed in an activity to see the cemetery himself, we yelled his name and pointed out the window.

"I'm impressed."

An October baby who conflated his birthday with Halloween the moment he could dress up like a witch, Nick's always been our most death-positive member of the family. He has a healthy relationship with the reaper, and this grisly game of car bingo was much more palatable than previous manifestations of his morbidity. He used to fantasize about dying so he could see Opa, and then play every single video game from the Sears holiday catalogue.

I always thought it was funny how much he rejoiced at the sight of even a single grave marker. Personally, I was always a little disappointed with the appearance of the hills and churchyards. Where were the jagged slate tablets I remembered from cartoons and Halloween-themed cereal boxes? Where were the overgrown mausoleums with glowing eyes shining from within? Every time I looked at one of Nick's impressive necropolises, I wanted something more dramatic, more theatrical. I wanted to look out the tinted window of Dad's Chevy and see a hand burst from the soil, exposed finger bones gleaming. I wanted Mom and Dad to scream, put the pedal to the metal, and call the Ghostbusters. I wanted a river of slime, a classic white-linen-with-eyeholes ghost, a werewolf with furry muscles ripping through its plaid flannel shirt.

Two horizons marked our imminent arrival in Bayfield. First, a hill, the kind so tall and gently sloped you almost forget you're driving upward at all, making the crest of it seem like the edge of a cliff, as if you are about to drive into the sky. But that's a false horizon, something you realize once you cross the threshold and begin the long, rolling descent to Lake Huron. You see the second edge farther off in the distance—a deep blue strip against the pale sky. Our destination was the shore of that infinite cobalt abyss.

From that hill, down to the land's terminus, we drove through a few small towns, each with its own gas station and church. Each with its own cemetery, sometimes two, every one prompting my brother: "I'm impressed."

I never went back to school to be a coroner. I wanted to, but not enough to overcome the stigma of earning the high school biology credits I'd neglected to pick up as a teen. I gave up on my childhood aspirations of professional medicine early, dropping biology in Grade 11 because I didn't like ecology. I just didn't care about animals. If I had my way, biology class would only look at human biology. I wanted to study people's bodies.

Encountering that closed door when I so urgently wanted an exit from my phone sales job put me in a dark place. Rent was starting to rise in Toronto, and I could sew a king-size quilt from all the playwriting grant rejection letters piling up on my desk. Instead, I supplemented my call centre work with a Starbucks job. I woke up at 5:00 a.m. to open the store alongside a senior employee, made lattes until the early afternoon, stumbled home to sleep three hours, and then headed downtown in time to interrupt people's dinners with a phone call, trying to convince them to buy tickets to Robert Lepage's production of *Bluebeard's Castle*. Oh, how I wished to be surrounded by corpses. Dead bodies don't tell you you're worthless for trying to make rent during a global recession. Dead bodies don't make byzantine custom latte orders because they think it's cute. Dead bodies get it—life's hard.

The thing that killed me most about my inability to become a coroner as I zombie-walked into the dark October of my mid-twenties was how much I'd come to love animals and ecology. I was a vegetarian. I was an evolution-obsessed new atheist. And—to the alarm of my friend Gwen, whose concerned gaze assessed my diminishing frame at a Halloween party—I was wasting away. "You look like hell," she said. "Are you dying?" It turns out the protein powder in complimentary Starbucks smoothies is not sufficient sustenance.

Animals teach us about death. You get a guppy or a hamster or a mouse, and it dies, and you see the false horizon, the hill before the water. You crest many hills before you even understand you're heading to the lake. You love something, you lose it forever, you see the blue band in the distance. You get used to the hills, passing cemeteries along the way as you finally find a better job, give up on ethical eating, abandon playwriting for something you can control a bit better. You long for rest, knowing it will come to you as it has for your friends, family, and starter pets. And then one day your cat dies and you realize just how naive you've been this whole damn time.

Animals play an important role in horror: they remove sin from the equation of death and suffering. Animals can't deserve the pain that humans justify spreading among themselves through narratives of projected guilt and mythologies of hubris. The deer clobbered at the beginning of Jordan Peele's movie *Get Out* didn't deserve it. Neither did Church from Stephen King's *Pet Sematary*. And certainly none of the creatures big and small in Nick Cutter's novel *The Troop* deserved their terrible fates. Cutter's Maritime contagion nightmare features scenes in which primate test subjects are exposed to the weaponized tapeworm that serves as the book's monster; the invertebrate eats them from the inside out like a rotting tree stump with arms, legs, and an anal itch that just won't quit. A psychopathic Boy Scout waterboards a cat in a bathtub, tears the legs off spiders, and crushes the black-orb eye of a crab between his finger and thumb. Worst of all, two young boys are forced to hunt a turtle for food, awkwardly stabbing it to death with a makeshift spear as it peeps in protest at their tearful execution.

The boys are already emotionally torn apart, having witnessed the brutal deaths of many infected humans, including their troop leader. As a reader, so have you. Yet the torture of the turtle is the most difficult part of the book to read. Unlike the annihilation of animals earlier in the novel, which foreshadow the sickening death to be visited on the human characters, the turtle's demise is a simple parable of cruelty. Those early-act cullings are guppies. The turtle is the family cat.

I have four little white paper squares stamped with black ink prints of my dead cat's paws. The vet sent them through the mail, tucked into a condolence card with a bunch of animal pictures on the front—a parrot, a guinea pig, a bunny rabbit, but no dog or cat. Clever.

"Sorry for your loss," it says. "Teddy was a sweet cat."

They were right about that. An orange long-haired tabby with green eyes, he loved to cuddle and kneaded the empty air in front of him if you rubbed his chest as he lay on his side. We adorned him with names: Ted, Tedster, Crumb, Theodore Hardbody McCrumb: Private Investigator. A perpetual goofball. All innocence. Except for the tumour deep in his torso.

"He's suffering," the doctor said in the dim examination room, lit only by the glow of Teddy's X-rays displayed on a computer monitor. The mass was the size of a tennis ball, white and impenetrable. It was the reason Teddy's kidneys were failing, why so many numbers on his medical charts were red instead of healthy black. So we did it there, in a room across the hall plastered with posters warning about the signs of pet obesity.

Emma and I were with Ted when it happened. The vet poisoned him in stages. His fearful, prolonged meows, the odour of the urine he leaked onto Emma's pants the last time she held him—he calmed down after the first shot, injected into the IV snaking from above his white paw. He breathed slower, and I felt the tension radiating from his body dissipate. We petted him. I want to say he kneaded the air, but I was too focused on his growing tranquility to notice what his little paws were up to. Those white fuzzy socks with pink pads.

The second shot stopped Teddy's heart. His pupils dilated and his lungs deflated. Frozen, he stared into a distance I couldn't fathom, beyond whatever false horizon I understand as the edge of existence. A small pool of blood collected under his nose.

I was angry. I was torn apart. And I wasn't alone. When we got in the car to drive home, empty cat carrier in the trunk, the radio started on ignition, playing "I Will Remember You" by Sarah McLachlan. Emma punched the dashboard controls. We drove home in the light rain, hating God. They call it pathetic fallacy because it's so unbelievably pitiful. A real hack move.

It cost a thousand dollars to kill Teddy and have his cremated remains disposed of in some massive pile of incinerated biowaste. I couldn't afford an urn. But the paw prints might be enough. Maybe some terrible ritual could make use of those dead-kitty finger paintings and make like a *Pet Sematary*, resurrecting my sweet boy, beating cancer in some biblical twist. It was a joke, I told myself, when I scrolled through Internet esoterica archives, hit Ctrl+F and searched the terms "resurrection," "feline," and "necromancy." But as I skimmed the lore and came up with nothing but witchy spells requiring blood from a cat's ear, I realized how willing I was to go the black-magic distance, to spit in the face of God and reverse Teddy's cruel fate. Even if it demanded human sacrifice. It's unpopular to admit, but I'm being emotionally honest when I say there are people in this world whose deaths I would gladly trade through some sort of blood magic if it meant I could have even a zombie version of Teddy back. The undead Crumb. Theodore reborn. Even today, when I look at those ink blots on my bookshelf, I can conjure a list of untypeable things I'm willing to do under a bad moon in a graveyard just to see those paws flex again, unsheathing white claws in defiance of Hades.

The desire for pet resurrection is high-level grief recovery with a practical bent. Pro-league pathos. It's all five stages you hear about in sitcoms and read about in self-help books, wrapped up into one transgressive wish. Denial that death must be permanent, anger at the so-called god who can't, as per *Pet Sematary*, "take his own cat," bargaining as you skim through old grimoires and check your weekly planner to take the requisite sick days to summon the right demon under the proper moon phase, depression as you realize the magnitude of your desperation, and, finally, acceptance that to make an undead abomination you might have to dig up a few corpses.

I discovered a lot about myself as I entertained the use of arcane arts to summon Teddy from the ash pile and start his heart pumping again. I learned I read horror a little too wishfully. I learned how much capacity I had to love an animal. I learned that crying in your early thirties still feels shameful, and I learned that the sympathy most people extend to those grieving a lost pet is equal to the sympathy they reserve for work colleagues getting over the flu. But chief among the lessons I learned was exactly how painful I find death. It was a surprise. Before I saw Teddy die, I thought I was a spooky person. I revelled in violent media, laughed at torture scenes in film, saw digital avatars made in my image perish to the point where witnessing my virtual demise became meditative. I daydreamed of giving eulogies. I thought I was used to permanent goodbyes. I pictured myself covered in the gore of an exhausting life, numb to the threat of the horizon.

But I hadn't seen the lake. It was a trick all along. Every funeral, all the gothic affectation and morbid contemplation—the fantasy career as a coroner, the absurd research into necromancy—those were false horizons, cresting hills, practice deaths, gentle upward slopes. Whether through his innocence or the insidious, creeping nature of his death, Teddy brought me to the terminal altitude, and I glimpsed that terrible blue in the distance. I saw how all that death I wrapped myself up in was just another way of living my life. Every corpse was another surrogate through which I could understand my own journey, passing cemeteries along the way to my final destination, doing my best to be impressed, and waiting for the screaming to stop.

ACKNOWLEDGEMENTS

This book was not my idea. Andrew Faulkner was a stranger when he emailed the contact address on my horror blog, asking if I'd be interested in writing an essay collection. He is a hell of an editor. With keen eyes and faithful conviction, he made my dream come true. Thank you, Andrew.

Publisher Leigh Nash deserves a heaping of praise too. This book is being published during a plague year. The fact that she perseveres in the face of viral human extinction inspires me to do good. If you see Leigh in the post-apocalyptic wastes, rally under her Invisible flag. Your life will be better. Thank you, Leigh.

Megan Fildes's reputation precedes herself in my household. One of the most exciting things about writing a book for Invisible was knowing that at the end Megan was going to design it. She did, and for that I am eternally grateful. Thank you, Megan.

Julie Wilson's boundless hustle and enthusiasm was apparent from the first time I met her at a Halifax poetry reading. Those qualities made working with her a joy and resulted in you holding this book right now. Thank you, Julie.

Some of the essays in this book are remixes and mash-ups of articles I wrote for *Everything Is Scary*. For years, I toiled away in that space with Tim Ford and Leslie Hatton, and I like to think we made something special out of it. Thanks, team.

To Alex Perala, my writer pal: thank you for the countless ethical hypotheticals, the opinions on unfinished work, and for your service. To Susan Stover, thank you for your encouragement, your fifteen years of friendship, and the endless puns. To John McKinnon, thank you for your consultation on music, and thank you for your invincible friendship. To Katie DuTemple and Andrea McCulloch, thank you for offering me love and support during the darker times described in this book, even if I didn't always accept it.

Thank you to Eugene Thacker, a person I never met, but whose *Horror of Philosophy* books helped me understand how to think about horror. Thank you to Michael Greyeyes, who taught me to think about performance, movement, tempo, and space. Thank you to Dr. Katherine Morris, who let me sit in on her lectures about vampires in history and culture. Thank you to Suzie Cochrane for telling me about the demon core. Thank you to Chris Deeves, who got me into metal. Thank you to Kevin Sealy, who taught me how to fight ghosts. Thank you to the Friday Night Fright Club, who remind me constantly that even the wildest horror stories can build communities of hope in dire times.

Thank you to John Semley, Paul Tremblay, and Meredith Graves for your kindness and generosity as readers.

My mom and dad, who continually cheer me on in all I do; my brother Nick, with whom I share a psychic connection; my partner Emma, whose creative soul inspires me to make and share, whose kindness fuels my empathy, whose love and support keep me breathing and writing—thank you all.

Finally, I was once told you should never thank the dead in print, but I have a debt to pay: Andrew Henderson is my stage manager.

INVISIBLE PUBLISHING produces fine Canadian literature for those who enjoy such things. As an independent, not-for-profit publisher, our work includes building communities that sustain and encourage engaging, literary, and current writing.

Invisible Publishing has been in operation for over a decade. We released our first fiction titles in the spring of 2007, and our catalogue has come to include works of graphic fiction and non-fiction, pop culture biographies, experimental poetry, and prose.

We are committed to publishing diverse voices and experiences. In acknowledging historical and systemic barriers, and the limits of our existing catalogue, we strongly encourage writers from LGBTQ2SIA+ communities, Indigenous writers, and writers of colour to submit their work.

Invisible Publishing is also home to the Bibliophonic series of music books and the Throwback series of CanLit reissues.

If you'd like to know more, please get in touch: info@invisiblepublishing.com